Famie's Adventures in Cooking

Sleeping Bear Press
310 North Main
P.O. Box 20
Chelsea, Michigan 48118
www.sleepingbearpress.com

Printed and bound in Canada by Friesens
10 9 8 7 6 5 4 3 2 1

Library of Congress Cataloging-in-Publication Data

Famie, Keith.
Famie's adventures in cooking / by Keith Famie
p. cm.
ISBN 1-886947-65-1
1. Cookery. I. Title: Adventures in cooking. II. Title.

TX714 .F34 2000
641.5—dc21

Check out Chef Famie's other adventures at www.famie.com

Famie's
Adventures
in Cooking

By Keith Famie

Food Photography By Joe Vaughn

Sleeping Bear Press

Table of Contents

Rainbow Connection

The Rainbow Connection is a Michigan nonprofit organization established in 1985. The mission of The Rainbow Connection is to grant wishes to children three to eighteen years old that have been diagnosed with life-threatening illnesses.

Many children have seen their dreams come true because of The Rainbow Connection. Some wishes that have been granted are computers, shopping sprees, an all-terrain wheel chair and the most requested wish of all—a trip to Disney World! The family is always included in these trips. Memories are so important!

Another component of The Rainbow Connection is their Wish Enhancement Program. This program is designed to provide fun opportunities to the wish child and their families after the wish has been granted. Enhancements have been tickets to sporting events, theater, the circus, and picnics. This program is supported by donations from individuals and corporations. Because we believe that laughter and happiness are very therapeutic, providing families with occasions to escape the burdens that accompany these awful illnesses is an important part of the mission of The Rainbow Connection.

All wishes are considered without regard to gender, race, or religious preference. Fundraisers and private donations support the organization.

A Board of Directors governs The Rainbow Connection. Under their direction is the Executive Director who is responsible for the overall operations and who is assisted by a multitude of volunteers.

The Rainbow Connection
14 W. Huron
Pontiac, MI 48342
(248) 338-7760

Sleeping Bear Press and Keith Famie will donate a portion of the proceeds from Famie's Adventures in Cooking to The Rainbow Connection.

This book is dedicated to my favorite two people, my children, Josh and Alicia.
They've always been supportive and happy to join me in the kitchen.

This book represents many years of cooking at stoves in restaurants, both in the United States and internationally. My experiences and more than 23 years in the world of food have been my passport around our planet. Ever since I can remember I've been fascinated with chefs and their ability to take raw fresh ingredients and turn them into edible works of art.

My styles have changed so much over the years—from the Chez Raphael days, influenced heavily by Nouvelle Cuisine, to Les Auteurs, which became the canvas for my culinary and entrepreneurial growth. Durango Grill was an escape from the intensity of high expectations that Les Auteurs required. More recently, as chef of Forte, I was able to fuse styles of cooking with places where I love to travel.

As I write this opening to this book by night, at day I'm planning 16 new locations that will be part of my series, "Famie's Adventures in Cooking," a collection of television shows based on Food Culture and Travel.

The recipes in this book are not complicated ones. I chose simple preparations that don't require many steps. I hope you enjoy these old standby recipes from days gone by.

Chez Raphael
The Early Years

In 1982, the Wisne Family made the decision to build a small, 42-seat restaurant in their newly constructed hotel, The Sheraton Oaks in Novi, Michigan. I was fortunate enough, age twenty-two, to be hired as the chef of this elegant restaurant. The Nouvelle Cuisine rage, driven by the great chefs from France, was in full force in the States. Everything I prepared was heavily influenced by the French cuisine. Maître'd Achille Bianchi and I made a great team. We ran the restaurant passionately. This dining mecca continued until the Wisne family decided to build a new and bigger restaurant next door. This grand establishment, four times the size of the original, was Chez Raphael. It was a dream come true.

Working with Achille for six years was a great experience. Every day presented a new adventure. Because the restaurant was so high-profile, we received requests for every imaginable event. One very memorable event occurred when a local businessman invited us to prepare a dinner feast for 100 of his closest friends. The dinner took place in a mansion on Lake Shore Drive in Grosse Pointe, Michigan. The host requested that the menu be authentic Eighteenth Century French style, with the wait staff dressed accordingly. Makeup and costumes transformed the staff. When the team was dressed for service that evening they were fully made up with white faces, long white wigs, white tights and puffy jackets. I chuckled all evening.

The Wisne family has continued to expand their restaurant business successfully. They now have four new restaurants, in addition to Too Chez (formerly Chez Raphael). Achille continues to hold court at Too Chez.

Above left: Achille in full uniform...doesn't he look marvelous?

The opening brigade of the new Chez Raphael.

Left: Maître'd Achille Bianchi and I await the evening's guests at Chez Raphael.

Bottom left: Rotisseried fresh duck.

Below: My handwritten chef's notebook. It contains some of my favorite recipes.

White Asparagus with Vinaigrette

White asparagus is produced by mounding dirt over the tops of asparagus during its growth period. The asparagus stays white due to its lack of exposure to the sunlight. This dish makes an ideal first course for any type of dinner, formal or otherwise.

24 fresh white asparagus spears
6 fresh green asparagus spears
    salt and pepper to taste
1 cup **Vinaigrette**

1. Trim the asparagus and peel the stem to remove any tough fibers.

2. In a large pot, bring water to boil. As soon as the water boils add a tablespoon of salt followed by the white asparagus. Boil for 5 minutes. Do not over-boil; asparagus spears should still be slightly "crunchy."

3. Blanch green asparagus for 2 minutes in a separate pan. Drain the asparagus and immediately submerge in a bowl of ice water to prevent further cooking. When cold, drain again.

4. Pat the white asparagus dry with paper towels and arrange on a serving platter. Drizzle with Vinaigrette. Garnish with green asparagus sliced into thin round pieces.

Vinaigrette

¼ cup red wine vinegar
1 cup olive oil
2 tablespoons Djon mustard
    salt & pepper to taste

Pour the vinegar into a medium bowl. Whisk in the olive oil and mustard until well blended. Season to taste.

Escargot with Prosciutto   Serves 4

I have prepared this recipe for 18 years. It is one of my favorites, not only because of the delicious combination of flavors, but also because it makes escargot lovers out of even the most reluctant diners.

2   tablespoons olive oil
½   small onion, diced
1   tablespoon garlic, chopped
2   cups button mushrooms, sliced
½   cup prosciutto, diced
24   small snails
1   cup port wine
¼   cup heavy cream
     salt and pepper to taste
2   cups chicken stock
1   cup bread crumbs
1   cup Asiago cheese, freshly grated
½   cup flat leaf Italian parsley, finely chopped
1   thinly sliced baguette

1. Preheat broiler.

2. In a large skillet, heat olive oil. Add onion, garlic, and mushrooms; sauté over medium heat until the onions are slightly brown, or caramelized, approximately 4 to 5 minutes.

3. Add the prosciutto and snails; sauté for 3 minutes. Stir in wine and cream. Simmer, stirring occasionally, until the liquid is reduced by half. Season with salt and pepper to taste. Remove the snails from the pan with a slotted spoon and set aside.

4. Add the chicken stock to the pan and simmer for 10 minutes. Return the snails to the pan; stir. Spoon the escargot mixture into a 9x9˝ ovenproof baking dish.

5. In a small bowl, mix the bread crumbs with the grated cheese and parsley. Distribute evenly over the escargot mixture. Place under a preheated broiler and broil until the top is golden brown, approximately 3 to 4 minutes. Serve on toasted baguette slices.

Wine Recommendation: Chianti

Chicken Breasts with Pear and Endive

4	boneless chicken breasts
½	cup flour
2	ounces olive oil
	salt and pepper to taste
2	tablespoons butter
2	heads Belgian endive, cleaned and diced
1	pear, cored and diced
1¾	cup chicken stock
1	cup heavy cream
¼	cup flat leaf parsley, chopped

1. Season chicken breasts with salt and pepper.

2. Dust the chicken breasts in the flour to coat; gently shake to remove excess.

3. In a large nonstick sauté pan, heat the olive oil over medium high heat. Add the chicken breasts and sauté for approximately 3 minutes on each side. Remove from pan, and keep warm until ready to serve.

4. In a saucepan, melt the butter over medium heat, add the endive and pear to the pan and sauté for approximately 5 minutes. Add the chicken stock and simmer until reduced by half. Add the cream and simmer until the sauce thickens and coats the back of a wooden spoon. Season with salt and pepper to taste. Stir in the parsley.

5. Place a cooked chicken breast on each serving plate and spoon the sauce over the chicken. Garnish with a sprig of fresh parsley.

Wine Recommendation: Pinot Noir

Grilled Marinated Duck Breast   Serves 2

If you love to grill, this is a great dish for a summer picnic. Just remember, game is best when sliced very thin before serving.

½   cup Chambord liqueur
1   teaspoon coarsely ground black pepper
1   tablespoon molasses
    juice of 1 orange
2   large, meaty duck breasts
1   cup chicken stock
    pinch of salt
1   tablespoon butter

Garnish

1½ cup zucchini, julienned
1½ cup butternut squash, julienned
14 melonball sweet potatoes
2   tablespoons butter
    salt and pepper to taste
2   sprigs of thyme

1. In a large stainless steel bowl mix together the Chambord, pepper, molasses and orange juice. Marinate duck breasts in Chambord mixture for approximately 40 minutes. Remove duck breasts and reserve the marinade.

2. Preheat grill. When hot, reduce heat to low.

3. Place the duck breasts on the grill. (Cook for approximately 3 minutes on each side for medium rare.) Remove from grill and let sit for several minutes before slicing.

4. Add ½ cup of the reserved marinade to a saucepan and over high heat, boil until reduced by half. Add the chicken stock and reduce for 5 minutes. Season to taste and whisk in butter.

5. To prepare garnish: Place zucchini and squash in a small pile in the middle of the plate. Arrange the sweet potatoes around the plate.

6. Slice the duck and fan it around the squash and zucchini. Ladle the sauce around the duck and garnish with a sprig of thyme. Serve immediately.

Wine Recommendation: Red Bordeaux

1. Peel sweet potatoes and using a melonballer, scoop out 14 sweet potato balls.

2. Blanch sweet potato balls in boiling water until halfway cooked, approximately 10 minutes.

3. In a hot sauté pan with 1 tablespoon of butter, add sweet potatoes and brown slightly. Season and reserve.

4. In another sauté pan with 1 tablespoon of butter, sauté the butternut squash and zucchini. Season and reserve.

Grilled Veal Chops with Wild Mushroom Polenta

Serves 4

This simple recipe turns these Grilled Veal Chops into an adventure for your mouth.

4   bone-in center cut veal chops (12 to 16 oz)

Marinade

1	cup olive oil
½	teaspoon chopped garlic
½	3-oz package sundried tomatoes
½	cup Balsamic vinegar
1	sprig basil
1	sprig Italian flat leaf parsley
1	sprig rosemary
3	sprigs English thyme
1	tablespoon fresh lemon juice
1	tablespoon Dijon mustard
2	Roma tomatoes, cut in half and grilled for garnish

1. Preheat broiler or grill.

2. Place all ingredients for marinade in blender and process until thoroughly mixed. Pour over veal chops and allow to marinate for 1 hour, turning occasionally.

3. Remove veal chops and brush off excess marinade.

4. Grill veal chops until done to desired temperature. While grilling, brush on marinade occasionally, taking care to avoid flare-ups. Serve with **Wild Mushroom Polenta** and grilled tomato.

Wine Recommendation: Barbera

Wild Mushroom Polenta

7	cups water
1	tablespoon salt
2	cups coarse cornmeal
2	tablespoons olive oil
4	oz oyster mushrooms, quartered
6	oz button mushrooms, quartered
4	oz dried porcini mushrooms, soaked in hot water, 15 minutes, drained and quartered
4	oz dried morels, soaked in water 15 minutes, drained and quartered
1	clove garlic, chopped
1	small leek, white part only, cleaned and diced
1	cup port wine
¼	cup chicken stock
2	tablespoons chopped fresh parsley
1	tablespoon chopped fresh thyme
½	cup mild Chevre cheese
½	cup Parmesan Reggiano cheese, freshly grated

1. Bring water to a boil in a large saucepan, add the salt and slowly pour in the cornmeal, stirring constantly to avoid lumps. Continue to boil for approximately 20 minutes, until the polenta pulls away from the spoon (if the heat is too low, the polenta will stew and not cook correctly). Add a little boiling water if the polenta sticks.

2. In a large sauté pan, heat the olive oil over medium high heat; add mushrooms and garlic and brown. Add the leek and cook until wilted. Pour the port wine over the mushrooms and stir; add the chicken stock and continue to simmer. Stir in the parsley and thyme.

3. Pour the polenta mixture over the mushrooms and mix well. Fold in the cheeses. Place in a stainless bowl and cover with plastic wrap until ready to serve.

Rosettes of Poached Salmon

Makes 8 to 10 rosettes

Your guests will think you're a genius when you serve these lovely salmon roses.

24 oz tail piece of salmon, skinned, pin bones removed
2½ cups **Nage Cooking Liquid**
3 tablespoons butter
1 cucumber, peeled, seeded and diced
1 cup tomato, skinned, seeded and diced
2½ cups heavy cream
1 tablespoon fresh dill, finely chopped
   salt to taste
2 tablespoons butter
2 sprigs of dill for garnish

1. Using a flexible slicing knife, working from the tail to the top of the filet, slice the salmon keeping the slices as thin as possible.

2. To form the rosettes: Roll the first slice of salmon around your finger. Continue to roll slice after slice around the first until you've accumulated 5 thin slices. It should look like a rose. Hold together with a tooth pick inserted through the bottom. Refrigerate the rosettes in a shallow roasting pan, leaving enough space between them so they do not touch.

3. When ready to prepare, pour the Nage Cooking Liquid around the salmon rosettes in the roasting pan. The liquid should cover the rosettes. Seal the pan with foil and cook on top of the stove over low heat, checking after 7 minutes. The salmon is done when it takes on an opaque rose color. Using a flat metal spatula, gently remove the rosettes from the pan and place them on a serving plate. Put a small pat of butter on each rose and wrap the plate with foil. This will keep the filets moist. Reserve the cooking liquid.

4. Sauté the cucumber and tomatoes in 1 tablespoon of the butter until they soften. Set aside. Add 2 cups of the reserved cooking liquid to a medium saucepan and heat to boiling. Continue cooking until liquid is reduced by half. Add cream and continue to cook until liquid becomes the consistency of a light sauce and coats the back of a spoon.

5. Add the reserved cucumber and tomatoes to the sauce, stir in the dill, and simmer gently for 1 minute, stirring constantly. Whisk in 2 tablespoons of butter to finish the sauce.

6. Divide the rosettes onto the 4 serving plates; ladle with sauce. Garnish with a fresh sprig of dill. Serve immediately.

Nage Cooking Liquid

1 cup red wine vinegar
1 cup white wine
½ cup water
1 stalk of celery, diced
1 carrot, diced
1 leek, thoroughly washed, diced

Mix all ingredients together.

Wine Recommendation: Pinot Noir

Sea Scallops with Saffron Chive Cream

Serves 4

12 large fresh Sea scallops
½ cup olive oil
 salt and pepper to taste
½ teaspoon saffron
1 cup + 1 tablespoon sweet vermouth
2 cups heavy cream
1 tablespoon butter
2 vine ripened tomatoes, peeled, seeded, and
  diced
1 teaspoon fresh chives, finely chopped
1 lb baby spinach
1 tablespoon butter
12 fresh green asparagus speers, peeled and
  blanched

1. Preheat broiler.

2. Place the scallops in a bowl with the olive oil and season with salt & pepper. Allow to marinate while you prepare the sauce.

3. Place the saffron and 1 tablespoon sweet vermouth in a small bowl and allow to steep until the liquid turns a bright yellow, about 10 minutes.

4. To prepare the Saffron Chive Cream: in a stainless steel saucepan, over high heat, boil remaining sweet vermouth until reduced by half. Slowly add the cream, in a steady stream, whisking constantly. Bring to a simmer and add the reserved saffron liquid. Continue cooking until the sauce coats the back of a spoon. Remove from heat and strain the sauce into another stainless steel pan. Bring to a simmer and whisk in the butter, tomatoes, and chives. Remove from heat. Keep warm until ready to serve.

5. Place scallops on a heat-proof tray and broil, turning once, until both sides are golden brown, approximately 4 to 5 minutes on each side.

6. Sauté the spinach in a hot sauté pan with butter until wilted. Reserve.

7. Divide the Saffron Chive Cream onto 4 plates. Place a small amount of the sautéed spinach in three separate places on the plate. Place a scallop on each mound of spinach. Garnish with asparagus and diced tomatoes. Serve immediately.

Wine Recommendation: Chablis

Grilled Tuna with Creole Sauce   Serves 4

This dish is great for lunch or dinner. The spicy sauce complements the tuna's tasty flavor. The tuna can be grilled or sautéed, whichever you prefer. If you do prefer to sauté, use olive oil instead of butter.

4	6-oz tuna steaks
½	onion peeled and julienned
1	red pepper, seeded and julienned
1	green pepper, seeded and julienned
1	yellow pepper, seeded and julienned
¼	cup olive oil
1	cup chili sauce
1½	cups canned beef broth
½	teaspoon minced garlic
½	teaspoon cumin
½	teaspoon cayenne pepper
	fresh chives, chopped, for garnish
2	cups thinly sliced, sautéed potatoes for garnish
20	slices zucchini, grilled

1. Preheat grill.

2. Sauté onions and peppers in olive oil until the onions are translucent, approximately 3 to 4 minutes. Add chili sauce and beef broth; mix thoroughly, adjusting temperature to medium. Add garlic, cumin, and cayenne pepper. Cook on low heat for about 10 minutes. Set sauce aside and keep warm.

3. Grill tuna to desired taste.

4. Place a tuna steak on each serving and ladle with Creole Sauce.

5. Garnish with chives and sautéed potato strips. Serve with grilled zucchini.

Wine Recommendation: Chablis

Les Auteurs

1988-1993

I wouldn't dream of beginning this chapter without immediately acknowledging two very special people: my General Manager Bruce Lilly and my Maître'd, Michael Morsette. Without the two of them, a great staff, and the support of my investors, we never would have accomplished so much. Our slogan was "Expect Something Different" and different we were! We operated the restaurant based on our sheer passion for good food and the finest service.

The name "Les Auteurs" simply means "the authors." It was my way of paying tribute to chefs and restaurateurs who had an impact on food and fine dining from as far back as my pre-school years. The walls were filled with photos and menus from restaurants all over the world. On one wall was a series of sketches that portrayed the history of cooking. We all had some great experiences during those years! We catered lunch for Presidents Bush and Ford. I was named one of "America's Best New Chefs" in 1989 by *Food & Wine* magazine and *Esquire* magazine designated Les Auteurs as one of "America's Best Restaurants." And there were many, many great dinners and special events at the restaurant. It was very exciting and never would have been possible without the dedicated and passionate work of a team of outstanding young people.

Les Auteurs was my canvas. I broke from my classical French cuisine training and explored new styles of cuisine. Inspired by Wolfgang Puck's success with Spago on the West Coast, I decided to recreate that style in Detroit.

One of my favorite things about Les Auteurs was "The Crayon Club." We always covered the tables with white butcher paper to give the room a crisp look and the diners something to doodle on. Each table had its own small box of crayons. Then one day, one of our regular customers, Peggy Daitch, brought her own box of 64 crayons with her and asked us to keep it in the office for her. When she came in for dinner she would ask for her crayons. After several weeks of frantically attempting to keep track of her crayons, we decided to form "The Crayon Club." We kept all the customer's crayons in a special place with their name on them, so they could use them whenever they came into the restaurant. It wasn't long before we had a "Crayon Vault," a glass cabinet displaying the boxes of crayons (with engraved plaques) for those individuals who had paid a one-time fee of $5. Les Auteurs served as a "canvas" for the community to express themselves while sharing a meal with family and friends. Among the many fabulous sketches, I treasure those drawn by two enormously talented artists, Richard Koslow and Robert Schefman. Thank you, Peggy, for bringing in that first box of crayons. You inspired something unique which will forever remain one of my fondest memories.

People ask me all the time if I'll ever reopen Les Auteurs and I always reply "Maybe... it's in my heart and soul."

A very warm thank you to everyone who worked there. Together, we helped set the pace for the restaurant trend in downtown Royal Oak.

Opposite page, bottom left: Mr. Ed Lundy and I, together we created Les Auteurs.

Opposite page, bottom middle: Don Tocco, myself, Bruce Lilly and Michael Morsette.

Opposite page, bottom right: Artist Richard Kozlow and I in front of the crayon drawings.

Left: Berlin Wall crayon drawing by Robert Schefman.

Black Bean Cakes with Smoked Turkey Makes approximately 16 small cakes or 6 to 8 large cakes

2   cups dry black beans*
¼   cup onion, finely chopped
½   stalk of celery, finely chopped
½   carrot, peeled and finely chopped
     pinch cayenne pepper
½   teaspoon cumin
½   jalapeño, washed and rinsed
     salt and pepper to taste
1   cup skinless smoked turkey, diced
2-4 tablespoons olive oil
     cornmeal for dusting
     fresh chives, sour cream or plain yogurt, salsa
       for garnish

1. Soak the dry beans overnight in enough water to cover beans with 2″ of water. The following day, drain and prepare as follows:

2. Place the beans, onions, celery, and carrot in a large stockpot. Add fresh water to cover. Bring to a boil. Reduce the heat and simmer until the beans are tender, about 1 to 1½ hours. Drain thoroughly. Place the bean mixture in a colander, set over a bowl, and cool in the refrigerator overnight to release as much liquid as possible.

3. The next day, place the bean mixture in a food processor fitted with the steel blade. Pulse until the mixture is coarsely ground. Do not purée.

4. Preheat oven to 350.°

5. Season the bean mixture with cayenne pepper, cumin, jalapeño, salt and pepper. Fold in the smoked turkey. Shape the mixture into cakes approximately 2″ in diameter and ½″ to ¾″ thick for appetizer-size servings or into 6 to 8 ounce round patties (about the size of a hamburger) for larger servings.

6. In a large saucepan, heat the olive oil over medium heat. Dust the patties lightly with cornmeal. Working in batches if necessary, add the patties to the skillet and brown on each side for approximately 2 minutes. Remove from the skillet and transfer to a baking sheet. Repeat with the remaining patties.

7. Place the patties in the oven and heat thoroughly, approximately 5-8 minutes. Remove from oven. Top with a dollop of sour cream or yogurt and a teaspoon of salsa and chives.

*Start the bean mixture for this recipe two days before you plan to serve it.

❦ *Wine Recommendation: Chardonnay*

Flank Steaks with Soy Ginger Marinade

Serves 2

This recipe was created for use with an inexpensive cut of meat commonly known as flank steak or London Broil. The Les Auteurs' lunch crowd loved it! The marinade tenderizes the meat and gives it an Asian flavor. An important technique to remember for serving this meat is to slice it thinly on the bias, thus ensuring tenderness.

1   cup soy sauce
1   teaspoon freshly grated ginger
2   tablespoons orange marmalade
1   clove garlic, minced
    juice of 1 lemon
    juice of 1 orange
½   cup olive oil
2   8-oz pieces flank steak
    Avocado Roast Corn Salsa, if desired

1. To prepare marinade: In a shallow bowl, whisk together the soy sauce, ginger, marmalade, garlic, lemon juice, orange juice, and olive oil.

2. Marinate the flank steak in the soy ginger marinade for one hour, turning once or twice. Grill the flank steaks to medium rare on a preheated grill.

3. Slice the steaks into thin pieces, on the bias, and serve with Avocado Roast Corn Salsa.

Avocado Roast Corn Salsa

1   ear grilled or oven roasted corn
1   ripe avocado, peeled and diced
2   Roma tomatoes, diced
1   small red onion, diced
1   tablespoon cilantro, chopped
¼   teaspoon cumin
    juice of 1 lime
¼   cup olive oil
¼   teaspoon cayenne
2   tablespoons rice wine vinegar
½   jalapeño pepper, diced (optional)

Slice the kernels off the ear of corn and place in a medium bowl along with the avocado, tomato, onion, and cilantro; stir. Add the remaining ingredients, and mix well. Cover the bowl with plastic wrap and refrigerate for 30 minutes.

 *Wine Recommendation: Red Zinfandel*

Fried Green Tomatoes with Sour Cream Horseradish Sauce   Serves 2

1   green tomato
     salt and pepper to taste
2   eggs
½   cup milk
1   cup all-purpose flour
1   cup cornmeal
¼   cup olive oil
     Sour Cream Horseradish Sauce
4 or 5 chives for garnish

1. Cut the tomato into 4 equal slices and season with salt and pepper.

2. In a medium bowl, beat the eggs with the milk until blended. Spread the flour on one plate and the cornmeal on another.

3. Dip the tomato slices in the egg mixture and then dredge in the flour. Dip again in the egg mixture, then dredge in the cornmeal. Repeat with the remaining tomato slices.

4. Heat the olive oil in a sauté pan, over medium-high heat, and brown the tomatoes well on each side.

5. Serve with Sour Cream Horseradish Sauce and garnish with chopped chives.

Sour Cream Horseradish Sauce

½   cup sour cream
½   cup nonfat plain yogurt
1   tablespoon horseradish
     juice of 1 lemon
½   cup cilantro, finely chopped

Mix all ingredients together in a small bowl. Refrigerate until ready to serve.

Lobster and Papaya Salad   Serves 4

This recipe is the result of a challenge to create a quick salad in a produce market on live television. It was delicious.

1	2½ lb lobster, boiled, meat removed, and chopped into ½″ pieces
1	ripe Ruby Red Papaya, peeled, seeded, and diced
1	small red onion, peeled and diced
1	jalapeño, seeded and diced
4	stalks of celery, cleaned and diced
8	sprigs fresh cilantro, finely chopped
2	blood or navel oranges, peeled and chopped
1	small head of Romaine lettuce, washed and sliced into thin ribbons
	celery leaves for garnish
	Honey Mustard Vinaigrette

1. Add the lobster, papaya, onion, jalapeño, celery, cilantro, and oranges to a medium bowl and toss gently to blend. Refrigerate until well chilled.

2. Place an equal amount of lettuce ribbons on each serving plate, top with the Lobster Papaya Salad, and drizzle with Honey Mustard Vinaigrette. Garnish with celery leaves. Serve immediately.

Honey Mustard Vinaigrette

¼	cup Honey Vinegar*
1½	teaspoons Dijon mustard
½	cup olive oil
3	oz walnut oil
¼	cup lowfat yogurt
	salt and pepper to taste

Place the vinegar and mustard in a blender. With the motor running, slowly add the oils, one at a time, in a steady stream, until well blended. Stir in the yogurt. Salt and pepper to taste. Store in refrigerator until ready to use.

*1 cup white wine vinegar and 2 tablespoons honey (can be kept in refrigerator for 2 weeks).

 *Wine Recommendation: Chardonnay*

Les Auteurs Meatloaf   Serves 6-8

One of my favorite customers, Laura Munder, gave this recipe to me and requested that I prepare it for a New Year's celebration at her home. I liked it so much I put it on the menu and it soon became one of the most popular items at Les Auteurs.

3	tablespoons unsalted butter
3	scallions, finely minced
1	small onion, finely minced
1	stalk of celery, finely minced
1	small carrot, finely minced
½	green pepper, finely minced
½	red pepper, finely minced
2	teaspoons garlic, minced
1	¾ lb lean ground beef
1	¾ lb sweet Italian Sausage, casing removed
1	teaspoon salt
¼	teaspoon cayenne pepper
1	teaspoon black pepper
1	teaspoon white pepper
½	teaspoon ground cumin
½	teaspoon ground nutmeg
½	cup half & half
½	cup catsup
3	large eggs, lightly beaten
¾	cup fine dry bread crumbs
	fresh sprigs rosemary, thyme, and basil for garnish

1. Preheat oven to 350.°

2. In a large nonstick sauté pan, melt the butter over medium heat. Sauté the scallions, onion, celery, carrot, peppers, and garlic until they are softened but not browned. Let cool. Set aside.

3. Combine the ground beef and sausage in a large bowl, mix well. Add the salt, cayenne, black and white pepper, cumin, and nutmeg. Add the reserved sautéed vegetables, half & half, catsup, eggs, and bread crumbs. Mix well.

4. Form the mixture into a loaf and place in a shallow baking dish or loaf pan.

5. Bake for 45 to 50 minutes. Remove from oven, drain excess fat, and let stand for 10 minutes. Slice. Garnish with rosemary, thyme, and basil. Serve with red skin (skins on) mashed potatoes, if desired.

 Wine Recommendation: Chianti

Porcino Dusted Halibut with Mustard Tomato Broth   Serves 4

1   cup shiitake mushrooms

¼   cup + 2 tablespoons olive oil
1   cup carrots, diced
1   cup white onion, diced
1   cup celery, diced
2   cups tomatoes, diced
1   cup tomato juice
½   cup whole grain mustard
1   quart water
       salt and pepper to taste
½   cup porcini mushrooms, finely ground in a
           coffee grinder
4   halibut filets, approximately 6 oz each
½   lb soba noodles, cooked
       Julienned Vegetable Garnish

1. Preheat oven to 350.°

2. Sauté shiitake mushrooms in 2 tablespoons olive oil
    until tender. Set aside.

3. To prepare the Mustard Tomato Broth, heat the
    remaining ¼ cup olive oil in a large saucepan and
    sauté the carrots, onion, and celery until the onion is
    translucent. Add the tomatoes, tomato juice, mustard,
    and water. Bring to a simmer and cook for 15 minutes.
    Strain into a medium saucepan and season to taste.
    Reserve liquid. Discard vegetables.

4. Spread the ground porcini on a large plate. Press one
    side of each halibut filet into the porcini to coat. Add a
    small amount of olive oil to a nonstick sauté pan, and
    over high heat, sear the halibut, porcini side down.

5. Place the filets, porcini side up on an ovenproof pan
    and cook in preheated oven for approximately 8 minutes.

6. Reheat the Mustard Tomato Broth. Place a small amount
    of soba noodles in each soup bowl. Place a filet of halibut
    on top of the noodles and ladle broth over all. Garnish
    with the shiitake mushrooms and Julienned Vegetable
    Garnish.

Julienned Vegetable Garnish

2   tablespoons olive oil
2   zucchini, julienned
1   carrot, julienned
2   leeks, julienned
2   stalks of celery, julienned

Sauté the vegetables in 2 tablespoons of hot olive oil, until
tender, approximately 3 minutes.

 *Wine Recommendation: Pinot Noir*

California Pizza

Makes one 8˝ pizza

Les Auteurs reflected the California food scene. This pizza accomplishes that in a scrumptious way. It was the best-selling item on the menu for years.

Cornmeal for work surface
1 8˝ round pizza shell (may use prepared pizza shell)
2 teaspoons pesto
1 teaspoon roasted garlic puree
3 oz **pizza sauce**
2 oz low-fat mozzarella cheese, shredded
½ oz Chevre cheese, crumbled
4-5 sundried tomatoes (oil packed), thinly sliced
6 cloves garlic, roasted
1 tablespoon freshly grated Parmesan cheese
fresh basil for garnish

1. Preheat oven to 500.°

2. Sprinkle cornmeal on work surface and place the pizza dough on the cornmeal.

3. Working quickly, spread the pesto, followed by the garlic puree and finally the pizza sauce over the dough. Top with mozzarella, Chevre, sundried tomatoes, and roasted garlic cloves. Carefully slide the pizza onto a preheated pizza tile and bake for 10-12 minutes until the crust is golden and the cheese is melted.

4. Remove the finished pizza from the oven, sprinkle with the Parmesan and fresh basil. Serve immediately.

Pizza Sauce

¼ cup tomato paste
1 cup crushed tomatoes
¼ cup fresh basil, chopped
1 clove garlic, chopped
1 tablespoons olive oil
salt to taste
pinch of cayenne pepper

In a blender, thoroughly mix all ingredients together. Let sit one hour before using.

Bruschetta with Tomato Relish

Serves 4

Everyone has a favorite version of Bruschetta with tomatoes, garlic, and basil. Here's a classic version; its bold flavors will whisk you away to Tuscany!

2 cups ripe tomatoes, seeded and chopped*
2½ teaspoons minced fresh garlic
3 tablespoons fresh basil, chopped
1 teaspoon kosher salt
¼ cup + 3 tablespoons extra virgin olive oil
8 ½˝ thick slices sourdough bread
¼ cup freshly shaved curls of Parmesan cheese
(Use a potato peeler to shave curls from a fresh piece of Parmesan.)

1. To prepare Tomato Relish: In a glass or stainless steel bowl mix together the chopped tomatoes, 1½ teaspoons of garlic, and the basil. Mix in salt and 3 tablespoons olive oil. Refrigerate.

2. Preheat grill or broiler.

3. Mix the remaining ¼ cup oil and 1 teaspoon minced garlic together. Brush both sides of the sourdough slices with the mixture. Grill or broil the slices for 1 to 2 minutes on both sides (be careful not to over-char the slices!)

4. Divide the toasted sourdough onto 4 serving plates, top with Tomato Relish and Parmesan curls.

Pumpkin Risotto with Pancetta and Chevre Cream   Serves 4

Autumn is my favorite season. I am always inspired to prepare something wonderful when the leaves begin to take on their new and brilliant shades of color. This recipe, an inspiration from years ago, combines the rich flavors of an American harvest with traditional Italian cuisine and delicate French cheese.

4   tablespoons olive oil
½   leek, cleaned and diced
1   cup shiitake mushrooms, julienned
½   cup pancetta, sliced into thin pieces (can
       substitute lean bacon or prosciutto)
½   cup flat leaf parsley, chopped
1   cup Arborio rice
3   cups hot chicken stock
½   cup canned pumpkin
     Chevre Cream
     seeds of 1 pomegranate (optional)

1. Heat 2 tablespoons of the olive oil in a sauté pan over medium high heat. Sauté the leeks and shiitakes until softened. In a separate sauté pan, add the pancetta and cook until crispy. In a small bowl, combine the leeks, shiitakes, crispy pancetta and parsley. Reserve.

2. To prepare risotto: In a saucepan, sauté the rice in the remaining olive oil for 3 to 4 minutes. Add 1 cup of the chicken stock, stirring continually. Add the remaining stock a little at a time, stirring continually, until it is absorbed. If rice is not fully cooked, add water, ¼ cup at a time, until thoroughly cooked.

3. When the risotto is finished, stir in the reserved leek mixture. Add the pumpkin and the Chevre Cream. Blend thoroughly. Risotto should be creamy. Continue stirring over low heat until desired serving temperature is reached.

4. Garnish with pomegranate seeds, if desired.

Chevre Cream

In a small saucepan, heat 2 cups of heavy cream. Stir in 6 oz of Chevre. Continue to cook, while stirring, until well blended, approximately 2 or 3 minutes. Remove from heat.

 Wine Recommendation: Chianti

Escalopes of Salmon Salad with Balsamic Vinaigrette   Serves 6

1   24 oz Norwegian Salmon
1   cup flour for dusting
¼   cup olive oil
1   lb assorted salad greens, washed and gently
       dried
l   large red onion, thinly sliced
4   vine-ripened tomatoes, thinly sliced
     Balsamic Vinaigrette
     salt and pepper to taste
1   baguette, thinly sliced and toasted

Balsamic Vinaigrette

1   cup olive oil
½   cup Balsamic vinegar
1   tablespoon water
1   tablespoon Dijon mustard
1   clove garlic, finely chopped
1   tablespoon sweet basil, chopped
1   tablespoon Italian flat-leaf parsley, chopped
     salt and pepper to taste

1. Cut the salmon into thin, flat (escalope) pieces. If necessary, wrap the salmon pieces in plastic wrap and pound with a wooden mallet until thin. Lightly coat the slices with flour, shaking off any excess.

2. In a nonstick sauté pan, heat olive oil. Over high heat, sauté the salmon escalopes for a few minutes; turn the slices over, and cook for a few more minutes until done, approximately 3 to 4 minutes.

3. Divide the salad greens onto six serving plates, top with onion slices and tomato.

4. Place an escalope of salmon on top of the greens. Drizzle lightly with Balsamic Vinaigrette. Add salt and pepper to taste. Serve with slices of baguette.

Place all ingredients in a blender. Mix at high speed until well blended.

Lobster Risotto with Lemon Grass Ginger Sauce   Serves 4

1   cup heavy cream
1   teaspoon fresh ginger, chopped
2   teaspoons fresh lemongrass, chopped
¼   cup olive oil
2   cups cooked whole lobster meat, diced
½   cup small morel mushrooms, if available
1   lb fresh shiitake mushrooms, cut in quarters
2   tablespoons flat leaf parsley, chopped
1   small white onion, diced
2   cups Arborio rice
7   cups chicken stock
    salt and pepper to taste
1   cup Parmigiano Reggiano, freshly grated
    flat leaf parsley for garnish

1. In a small saucepan over medium to low heat, simmer the heavy cream, ginger, and lemongrass for 5 minutes. Strain through a fine sieve into a small bowl. Reserve cream.

2. Add 2 tablespoons of olive oil to a medium sauté pan. Add the lobster, morels, and shiitake mushrooms; brown slightly. Stir in the chopped parsley and remove from heat.

3. Heat the remaining olive oil in a deep stainless steel saucepan. Add the onion and cook over medium heat until translucent. Add the rice and stir continuously for 2 minutes. Add half of the chicken stock and cook, stirring continually with a wooden spoon. When the stock is absorbed, add the remaining chicken stock, 1 cup at a time, continuing to stir until all of the stock has been absorbed. The risotto is done when all of the liquid has been absorbed and the rice is cooked but still slightly firm.

4. Add the cream mixture, lobster, and shiitake mushrooms and cook for an additional 5 minutes, stirring continually. Risotto should be creamy. If needed, add a small amount of water. Season with salt and pepper to taste.

5. Serve on leaves of spinach. Garnish with freshly grated Parmigiano Reggiano and sprigs of flat leaf parsley.

Wine Recommendation: Chardonnay

Green Pumpkin Seed Encrusted Whitefish with Fennel Onion Compote   Serves 4

4   6-oz whitefish filets
½   cup Mexican green pumpkin seeds, roughly
      chopped (also know as pepitas)
1   fennel bulb, cleaned and sliced into ½″ pieces
½   cup red onion, diced
¼   cup honey
2   bay leaves
½   cup Spanish vinegar*
      salt and pepper to taste
½   cup olive oil
4   **tomato halves, confited**
1   tablespoon Italian flat leaf parsley, chopped

1. Spread the chopped pumpkin seeds on a sheet of waxed paper. Gently press the whitefish filets, skinless side down, into the pumpkin seeds. Set aside.

2. To prepare Fennel Onion Compote: In a medium saucepan, cook the fennel at a low simmer with the red onion, honey, bay leaves, vinegar, salt and pepper for approximately 20 minutes, until the fennel is cooked to a tender crisp. Keep warm until ready to serve.

3. Preheat oven to 400.°

4. In a nonstick sauté pan, heat the olive oil over medium–high heat and brown the filets, seed side down. When they are golden brown, transfer to a sheet pan, lined with aluminum foil, and bake for approximately 10 minutes in the oven.

5. Sprinkle each filet with parsley. Place a filet on each serving plate and top with Fennel Onion Compote. Serve immediately.

* Spanish vinegar is readily available from Mediterranean Specialty Markets.

❧ Wine Recommendation: Chardonnay

Confit of Tomatoes

2   Roma tomatoes, cut in half
      extra virgin olive oil, to cover halfway
3   cloves garlic, peeled
      salt and pepper

1. Preheat oven to 300.°

2. To confit the tomatoes, place the halved tomatoes cut side down in an ovenproof baking dish.

3. Add olive oil until it covers tomatoes halfway.

4. Add the garlic cloves.

5. Cover dish with aluminum foil and place in oven.

6. When tomatoes begin to get tender, turn them over and continue cooking. Tomatoes are finished when soft.

Shrimp Pasta with Horseradish Dill Sauce

Serves 4

 2 cups heavy cream
 1 tablespoon fresh horseradish
 1 lb fusilli pasta (or similar curly pasta)
 2 tablespoons olive oil
 1 lb Gulf shrimp, peeled, deveined and split in half
 8 large button mushrooms, sliced
 6 sundried tomatoes, packed in oil, or softened
   in warm water if dried
 1 teaspoon dill, chopped
   salt and pepper to taste
 1½ lbs fresh spinach, washed and spun dry
   Parmigiano Reggiano or Asiago cheese, freshly
   grated

1. Combine the cream and horseradish. Bring to a boil over medium high heat. Strain through a fine sieve and reserve.

2. Cook the fusilli according to directions on package. Drain. Keep warm.

3. Place the olive oil in a medium-sized sauté pan. Sauté the shrimp in olive oil until done, approximately 3 minutes. Remove the shrimp from the pan and reserve.

4. In a large nonstick sauté pan, brown the mushrooms over high heat.

5. Add the cooked shrimp to the pan with the mushrooms. Stir in the sundried tomatoes, dill, and reserved cream mixture and cook at a low simmer for 3 minutes. Season with salt and pepper.

6. Toss the cooked pasta with the shrimp sauce in a large bowl. Add the spinach leaves, toss again, and top with the grated cheese. Serve immediately.

Wine Recommendation: Chablis

Coconut Fried Shrimp with Honey Mustard Mayonnaise

Serves 2

I was inspired to create a new dish by the warm tropical climate while a guest chef aboard the Sea Goddess on a cruise to the Caribbean Islands. Coconuts were abundant so I decided to use them in this sizzling dish. It's as easy as 1–2–3 to prepare!

1	cup grated dried coconut
3	tablespoons curry powder
1	tablespoon tumeric
1	tablespoon ground cumin
4	egg whites
10	large Gulf shrimp, peeled and deveined with tails
	fresh chives, for garnish

1. Mix all of the dry ingredients together.

2. Place egg whites in a small, shallow bowl and whip for 30 seconds with a wire whip to froth. Dip the shrimp into the egg whites, then into the coconut mixture. Place on a sheet of waxed paper.

3. In a large nonstick skillet or frying pan, heat the oil. Carefully add the shrimp and sauté until golden brown, approximately 5 minutes. Work in batches, if necessary, taking care not to overcrowd the pan.

4. Serve with Honey Mustard Mayonnaise. Garnish with chives

Wine Recommendation: Chardonnay

Honey Mustard Mayonnaise

Stir together:
- ½ cup mayonnaise
- ¼ cup honey
- 2 tablespoons Dijon mustard

Harvest Butternut Squash Soup

Serves 4

This was the most requested soup at Les Auteurs. Each year when autumn neared and the leaves changed colors it was as if a signal was sent to all of our patrons. They would call to see if this soup was on the menu yet and then they'd begin stopping in—just for the soup. I realize now how much these simple dishes meant to so many people. Those were the days…

3   lbs butternut squash, halved and seeded
1   stick butter, cut into small pieces + 2 tablespoons butter
2   leeks, cleaned
     cornmeal for dusting
     salt and pepper to taste
3   tablespoons olive oil
2   carrots, diced
2   stalks of celery
½   onion, diced
1   small shallot, minced
¼   teaspoon allspice
¼   teaspoon orange zest
2   quarts chicken stock
1   tablespoon flat leaf parsley, for garnish

1. Preheat oven to 350.°

2. Place the squash halves on baking sheet. Cut one stick of butter into small pieces and scatter over squash. Season with salt & pepper and bake for 45 minutes or until flesh is soft. Remove from oven and allow to cool. Remove the skin. Chop into small pieces and set aside.

3. Meanwhile, drizzle water over the leeks. Coat lightly with cornmeal. Sauté in 2 tablespoons butter until they begin to turn a golden brown. Remove from heat and place on paper towel. Season with salt and pepper.

4. In a large stockpot, sauté carrots, celery, onion, shallot, allspice, and orange zest in butter for 10 minutes. Add the chicken stock and simmer for 10 minutes. Add the reserved butternut squash and simmer for an additional 10 minutes. Remove from the heat and strain into a large stockpot. Reserve liquid.

5. Add the strained vegetables, in batches, to a food processor and purée, returning the puréed vegetables to the reserved liquid.

6. After all of the vegetables are puréed and returned to the liquid, whisk with a wire whip until the mixture is smooth and well blended. Season with salt and pepper and heat until desired temperature for serving.

7. Ladle the soup into bowls and top with chopped parsley and sautéed leeks. Serve immediately.

🍇 *Wine Recommendation: Sherry*

Grilled Vegetable Soup   Serves 4

Grilled vegetables are an essential flavor in this soup. It's a great way to make use of any leftover vegetables from last night's barbecue, or you can sub-
stitute whatever vegetables you have on hand. Serve with crunchy bread for a quick, delicious dinner.

1	8-oz can tomato soup, diluted according to directions
2	10-oz cans V-8® Juice
1	medium zucchini, grilled and diced
1	small eggplant, grilled and diced
1	red pepper, grilled and diced
1	yellow pepper, grilled and diced
8	scallions, grilled and diced, half reserved for garnish
	kernels from 1 grilled ear of corn
6	Calamata olives, pitted and chopped
¼	cup chopped fresh basil
1	teaspoon cayenne pepper
1	teaspoon cumin
4	leaves of fresh basil, sliced into thin ribbons, for garnish
4	fresh chives, chopped, for garnish
1	avocado
	salt and pepper to taste

Place all ingredients in a large saucepan and stir to blend. Bring to a simmer and cook for 15 minutes. Garnish with grilled scallions, ribbons of fresh basil, chives, and slices of avocado. Season to taste. Bon Appetit!

Durango Grill

"Where the Cowboys Came to Roam"

Everyone pretty much thought that I had been kicked in the head by a wild horse when I announced the concept of Durango Grill. It was 1993 and my dream restaurant, Les Auteurs, was struggling after five years. I had a lot of ideas simmering on the stove about what to do with Les Auteurs. It needed a drastic change.

I had taken a trip out West a few years prior to this time and had fallen in love with a little town in southwestern Colorado called Durango. It was kind of a cross between a cowboy town and mountain land all in one. I recalled how much fun I had on the trip and how fabulous it would be to recreate the same atmosphere at home. I was inspired! I knew it would be fun for adults and children, as well as the staff.

With a great deal of help from my good friend, restaurant kitchen designer, Ed Whitney, we set out to bring the West to Royal Oak, Michigan. From the ironwood branded floors to the Indian mural on the wall and a real stuffed buffalo head, it was authentic. Shoot, we even had a little train running around the bar.

My General Manager, John Messina, acted as Marshal in the front of the house. The rest of the staff wore cowboy gear. The fact Les Auteurs had been transformed into a cowboy restaurant was the talk of the town!

It was unbelievable fun. The food was served cowboy style and we made certain that the patrons could smell the fragrance of smoke and burning wood wafting in from the kitchen. We played old cowboy movies on TV and country music provided the background. Everyone had a "rootin' tootin'" good time. I even walked the dining room in spurs!

Here are some of Durango Grill's best recipes for you to rustle up at home.

Left: Our new sign and new interior. We were ready for business.

Below: Horses in front of the restaurant became a common occurance. My children, Josh and Alicia loved it.

Black Bean Soup with Durango Salsa and Avocado Cream

Serves 4

1 cup black beans
2 stalks of celery, diced
1 carrot, diced
1 white onion, diced
2 tablespoons olive oil
6 cups chicken stock
½ teaspoon cumin, ground
   salt and pepper to taste
   Durango Salsa
   Blue corn chips
   Avocado Cream

1. Soak the black beans in water overnight. Drain and set aside.

2. Sauté celery, carrot, and onion in olive oil until tender, approximately 3 minutes. Add black beans and chicken stock. Bring to a boil, reduce heat and simmer until beans are tender, approximately 1½ to 2 hours.

3. Transfer the bean mixture to a blender or food processor, in batches, and purée. Return mixture to stockpot. Stir in cumin. Season with salt and pepper.

4. Arrange several blue corn chips on top of individual servings of soup. Top with a dollop of Durango Salsa. Drizzle with Avocado Cream. Serve immediately.

Durango Salsa

1 cup canned diced tomatoes, with juice
1 small red onion, diced
¼ cup finely chopped cilantro
1 medium-size tomato, seeded and diced
1 jalapeño, roasted and diced
   juice of 1 lime
2 tablespoons olive oil
2 or 3 teaspoons hot sauce
   salt and pepper to taste

Mix all of the ingredients in a large bowl. Allow to rest in the refrigerator for several hours before serving.

Avocado Cream

1 ripe avocado, seeded and removed from skin
1 tablespoon cilantro, chopped
   juice of 1 lime
½ cup sour cream
1 tablespoon plain yogurt

Purée the avocado, cilantro, lime juice, sour cream, and yogurt in a blender or food processor. Pour into a squeeze bottle and set aside until ready to serve.

Buffalo Burgers

Serves 4

I could have hung a sign at Durango Grill that read, "10,000 Buffalo Burgers Sold and Counting!" Once someone tried one, they were hooked. Buffalo meat is leaner than beef and higher in protein. You have to add something to it to give it moisture, so I used canned green chiles.

2	lbs ground buffalo meat
1	8-oz canned green chiles, drained and diced
1	teaspoon cayenne pepper
1	teaspoon cumin
1	tablespoon salt
	Famie's Simple and Spicey BBQ Sauce
1	red pepper, roasted, peeled, seeded and julienned
	Avocado Roast Corn Salsa
	salt and pepper

1. Preheat grill or broiler.

2. In a large bowl, mix the first five ingredients together until well blended. Refrigerate until ready to use.

3. Form into 4 large patties, place on grill and cook to desired taste.

4. Season with salt and pepper to taste, place on hamburger buns. Top with roasted red peppers and Famie's Simple and Spicey BBQ Sauce. Serve with Avocado Roast Corn Salsa.

Famie's Simple and Spicey BBQ Sauce

1	chipotles in adobe sauce
8	oz of your favorite smokey BBQ sauce

Blend together in a small bowl. Store in the refrigerator.

Avocado Roast Corn Salsa

2	ears of grilled or oven-roasted corn
2	ripe avocados, peeled and diced
5	Roma tomatoes, diced
1	small red onion, diced
1	tablespoon cilantro, chopped
½	teaspoon cumin
	juice of 1 lime
½	cup olive oil
½	teaspoon cayenne
¼	cup rice wine vinegar
½	jalapeño pepper, diced (optional)

Slice the kernels off the ear of corn and place in a medium bowl with the avocado, tomato, onion, and cilantro; stir. Add the remaining ingredients and mix well. Cover the bowl with plastic wrap and refrigerate for 30 minutes.

Chicken Fried Steak   Serves 4

4   steaks of choice, approximately 7-oz
    salt and pepper to taste
2   cups lowfat buttermilk
2   cups dried cornbread crumbs
1   cup olive oil
1   teaspoon dried parsley flakes
    Cilantro Lime Sauce (recipe on page 70)
    Pinto Cowboy Beans

1. Lightly pound the steaks with a meat tenderizer until they are thin. Season with salt and pepper.

2. In a medium bowl, soak the steaks in the buttermilk.

3. Spread the cornbread crumbs on a large plate and dredge the steaks in the cornbread crumbs to coat completely.

4. In a large nonstick sauté pan, heat the olive oil over medium heat. Add the steaks, turning to brown on both sides. Cook to desired taste.

5. Serve on a bed of Pinto Cowboy Beans. Drizzle with Cilantro Lime Cream Sauce.

Pinto Cowboy Beans

1   cup pinto beans
½   cup olive oil
2   cloves garlic, minced
1   onion
1   stalk of celery, diced
1   small carrot
2   roma tomatoes, diced
½   teaspoon dried oregano
½   teaspoon ground coriander
1   canned Chipotle pepper, diced*
1   small red bell pepper, roasted, seeded & diced
1   small yellow pepper roasted, seeded & diced
6   cups chicken stock

1   tablespoon hot sauce
    juice of 2 limes
½   cup cilantro, chopped
    salt and pepper to taste

1. Rinse pinto beans thoroughly under cold water. Carefully check beans to make certain they are clean prior to using.

2. Place pinto beans in a large pot and cover with water. Cook for 2 and a half hours on medium heat until beans are soft but not mushy.

3. Strain and set aside.

4. In a 3 qt. stainless saucepan heat ½ cup olive oil. Sauté garlic, onion, celery and carrots until onions are translucent, approximately 3 to 4 minutes.

5. Add tomatoes oregano, coriander and continue to cook for an additional 3 minutes.

6. Add beans and peppers, including the chipolte. Sauté for 2 minutes.

7. Add all other ingredients, except cilantro, and allow to simmer for 15 minutes. Add cilantro and season to taste just before serving.

canned chipotle peppers are generally packed in adobe sauce and can be found in specialty markets

 *Wine Recommendation: Cabernet Sauvignon*

New Mexico Mesa Chicken Rollups

Serves 4

I made this at a picnic on a mesa in New Mexico. Simple to do but "gourmet" in flavor.

1	cup goat cheese
½	cup sun-dried tomatoes
4	flour tortillas
4	grilled boneless, skinless chicken breasts, thinly sliced
2	ripe avocados, peeled and sliced
	Durango Salsa
2	cups assorted salad greens, washed and dried
	Smoky barbecue sauce—your favorite brand

1. In a small bowl, blend the goat cheese with the sun-dried tomatoes. Spread a little of the goat cheese mixture on each tortilla. Distribute the chicken, avocado, Durango Salsa, and greens over each tortilla.

2. Add a little of your favorite barbecue sauce, roll up the tortillas and serve with corn chips, if desired. Mmmmmmmmmm!

Durango Salsa

1	cup canned diced tomatoes, with juice
1	small red onion, diced
¼	cup finely chopped cilantro
1	medium-size tomato, seeded and diced
1	jalapeño pepper, roasted and diced
	juice of 1 lime
2	tablespoons olive oil
2 or 3	teaspoons Tabasco® sauce
	salt and pepper to taste

Mix all of the ingredients in a large bowl and allow to rest in the refrigerator for several hours before serving.

 Wine Recommendation: Red Zinfandel

Trout in a Bag

Serves 2

Trout in a Bag was designed with fly–fishing campers from out West in mind. We kept a trout tank in the middle of the restaurant with a sign over it that read: "You pick 'em, we stick 'em". This entire dish is prepared in a brown paper bag.

2	12 to 16-oz whole trout, boned, heads removed
	salt and pepper to taste
1	small white onion, sliced
1	tablespoon fresh basil, chopped
4	mushrooms, sliced
1	medium tomato, seeded and diced
2	tablespoons butter, cut into small pieces
1	lemon, sliced in half
1	tablespoon chopped dill
2	brown paper bags

1. Preheat oven to 350.°

2. Season the inside of the trout with salt and pepper. Sprinkle the onion, basil, mushrooms, and tomato over each trout; top with pieces of butter, squeeze the juice from one-half lemon over each and sprinkle with dill. Carefully slide each trout into its own paper bag and tightly roll up the end of the bag.

3. Place each of the bags on a sheet pan and bake in the oven for 15 to 20 minutes.

4. Remove from oven, place each bag on a serving plate, slice the bag open through the center, and fold back the sides.

Wine Recommendation: Sauvignon Blanc

Broiled Jalapeños with Jack Cheese

Serves 2

While visiting my good friends Kevin and Karen (Midwesterners who transplanted themselves to Albuquerque, New Mexico), I came across this dish. It was truly a case of love at first bite! For me, there's nothing more relaxing than to sit back with a plate of these and an ice-cold Corona. The Jack cheese and the yogurt help to neutralize the heat from the jalapeños.

6   fresh jalapeños, split in half and seeded*
1   cup Jack cheese, freshly grated
    Cilantro Lime Sauce
    cilantro chopped for garnish

1. Preheat the broiler for 10 minutes.

2. Place the jalapeños on a sheet pan, inside facing up. Broil for 2 minutes.

3. Remove from the broiler, sprinkle with cheese, and return to the broiler until the cheese fully melts, 3 to 4 minutes.

4. Remove from broiler, drizzle with Cilantro Lime Sauce, sprinkle with chopped cilantro and enjoy!

* If your skin is sensitive to heat, wear rubber gloves when working with hot peppers.

Cilantro Lime Sauce

½   cup plain yogurt
½   cup sour cream
    juice of 1 lime
½   cup cilantro, chopped
    pinch cayenne pepper

In a small bowl, blend all ingredients with a wire whisk. Chill until ready to serve.

Know Your Chiles

Bell Pepper . . . . . no heat
Ancho . . . . mild, sweet
Poblano . . . . ranges from mild to spicy
Jalapeño . . . . ranges from moderately hot to very hot
Chipotle . . . . dried smoked jalapeño, flavor hints a little of chocolate
Serrano . . . . extreme heat
Habañero . . . . . . 50 times hotter than the jalapeño

F.Y.I. Human beings are the only creatures on the planet to eat chiles! The heat in the skin of the chiles is actually their defense mechanism.

Cedar Plank Vegetable Platter   Serves 2

This is it right here — the best vegetable platter you will ever taste! It is a perfect blend of the cedar flavor from the wood mingled with the sweet taste of Balsamic vinegar and olive oil. You'll need piece of cedar wood about 10″ long and 6″ wide.

1	10″ x 6″ piece of cedar
1	ear of corn, sliced into ½″ round pieces
1	carrot, peeled and sliced
2	portobello mushrooms, thickly sliced
4	shiitake mushroom caps
½	red pepper, julienned
1	stalk of broccoli, cut in half lengthwise
4	pea pods
1	Roma tomato, cut in half lengthwise
4	spears of asparagus
1	stalk of celery
1	small bunch spinach
	salt and pepper to taste
	Marinade
	Cilantro Lime Sauce

1. Completely submerge cedar in water overnight.

2. Preheat oven to 400.°

3. Place all of the vegetables, except for the spinach, in a large bowl. Pour the marinade over the vegetables and marinate in refrigerator for approximately 4 hours. Stir occasionally to mix.

4. Arrange the spinach leaves on a piece of cedar plank, distribute the vegetables over the spinach, and season with salt and pepper.

5. Bake the vegetables on the cedar plank in the oven for 20 minutes. Remove from oven. Drizzle with Cilantro Lime Sauce and serve.

Marinade

1	cup olive oil
½	cup Balsamic vinegar
1	tablespoon chopped garlic
½	cup chopped fresh basil
½	cup chopped flat leaf parsley
2	sundried tomatoes packed in oil

Combine all ingredients in a blender or food processor and pulse until well blended.

Cilantro Lime Sauce

¼	cup plain yogurt
¼	cup sour cream
	juice of 1 lime
½	cup chopped cilantro
	pinch cayenne pepper

In a small bowl, blend all the ingredients with a wire whisk. Chill until ready to serve.

Famie's Branding Hot Buffalo Chili

This was by far one of the most requested items at Durango Grill. The delicious taste of the buffalo combined with the intense flavor of the Chili Puree make it a treat you'll want again and again. We typically served it in hollowed out sourdough rolls. I liked it topped off with melted Mozzarella and cheddar cheeses. By the way, if you ever enter a chili cook-off, I suggest you use this recipe. I bet you win!

3   lbs ground buffalo
1   lb hickory smoked bacon, diced
2   white onions, diced
1   stalk of celery, diced
20   baby corn ears, cleaned & rough cut
2   red peppers, roasted, seeded & diced
2   yellow peppers, roasted, seeded & diced
6   Roma tomatoes, diced
1   teaspoon cumin
1   tablespoon oregano
1   tablespoon chili powder
½   cup brown sugar
⅔   cup flour
½   cup olive oil
16   oz Honey Brown® beer
16   oz canned tomatoes
16   oz V8® juice
16   oz canned tomato sauce
  several sprigs cilantro, chopped for garnish
  Mozzarella cheese, grated
  cheddar cheese, grated
  Chili Puree

1. Prepare Chili Puree. Set aside.

2. In a 2 gallon stainless steel pot, brown the bacon. Drain. Add buffalo and brown.

3. Add vegetables, dry ingredients and olive oil. Cook until onions are translucent, approximately 15 minutes, on medium-high heat, stirring not to burn.

4. Add Chili Puree, beer, canned tomatoes, V-8® juice, water, and canned tomato sauce; simmer on low heat for 25 minutes.

5. Just before serving, sprinkle a little freshly chopped cilantro into the bottom of each bowl. Note: if not using sourdough rolls, use oven proof bowls if you wish to melt cheese on top of chili.

6. Top with grated Mozzarella and cheddar cheese. Arrange on a sheet tray and place under broiler for 2 to 3 minutes or until cheese melts and bubbles.

Chili Puree

1   oz Anaheim dried chili pepper*
¼   oz dried habanero chili pepper*
6   cloves garlic, chopped
4   jalapeños, pre roasted, skinned & seeded
2   fresh cayenne peppers, roasted, skinned & seeded
1   cup water
1   cup Balsamic vinegar
1   tablespoon salt

In a saucepan over medium heat, add all ingredients and simmer for 2 minutes. Transfer to a blender and process until smooth.

*Dried chilies can be purchased at Mexican food stores or at your local specialty market. If unable to locate, you may substitute fresh roasted peppers, peeled & seeded. Caution: habanero peppers are very hot.

Stuffed Mammoth Potato
Serves 2

Durango Grill was home to all of the Michigan cowboys and the Stuffed Mammoth Potato. We served many of these on a busy Saturday night.

2 large baking potatoes
1 cup Buffalo Chili (see page 74)
2 6-oz boneless, skinless chicken breasts,
    grilled and sliced
8 broccoli florettes, blanched
4 button mushrooms, sliced & sautéed
1 cup Monterey Jack cheese, shredded
4 pickled jalapeños, sliced
   Durango Salsa
   Cilantro Lime Sauce

1. Preheat oven to 350°.

2. Wash potatoes and dry thoroughly. Brush potato skins with a little olive oil and bake until done. To test for doneness, squeeze potatoes gently, if they feel soft inside they are cooked completely or insert a toothpick in the center; if it comes out clean the potato is done.

3. Remove potatoes from oven and cut a deep pocket into each potato. Squeeze potato from ends to create a wide enough pocket to allow room for fillings.

4. Place potatoes in an ovenproof baking dish. Ladle Buffalo Chili into potato pockets. Top with chicken slices, broccoli, mushrooms and Monterey Jack cheese. Place the jalapeños on top of the cheese and bake in oven for approximately 10 minutes, until the cheese is completely melted. Remove from oven.

5. Prior to serving, spoon Durango Salsa over each potato and drizzle* with Cilantro Lime Sauce.

An easy technique for drizzling is to place the sauce in a squirt bottle. Great for leftover storage, too.

Durango Salsa

1 cup canned diced tomatoes, with juice
1 small red onion, diced
¼ cup finely chopped cilantro
1 medium tomato, seeded and diced
1 jalapeño, roasted, peeled and diced
   juice of 1 lime
2 tablespoons olive oil
2 to 3 teaspoons hot sauce
   salt and pepper to taste

Mix all of the ingredients in a large bowl and allow to rest in the refrigerator for several hours before serving.

Cilantro Lime Sauce

½ cup plain yogurt
½ cup sour cream
   juice of 1 lime
½ cup cilantro, chopped
   pinch cayenne pepper

In a small bowl, blend all ingredients with a wire whisk. Chill until ready to serve. If desired, use a blender or food processor.

On The Road

Michigan Visits Paris and China

I have a philosophy…"You really haven't been there until you've eaten the food."

I have been traveling the globe in search of grand adventures and exotic food since the age of nineteen, when one day I jumped on a plane headed for France. I left Michigan brimming with hope that once I arrived in the land of majestic cuisine

I, too, would be able to create these wondrous foods. Then before I knew it, I was in Monte Carlo. Thus began my international adventures in cuisine. While in Europe, not only did I learn a tremendous amount about the preparation of foods, I also learned many life lessons, which I carry with me to this very day. Since that time I have traveled the world in my quest for culinary adventures.

Three events that hold special meaning for me are the Michigan Lunch in Paris, the Michigan Dinner in China, and a documentary I filmed in Vietnam (Please refer to the Vietnamese chapter on page 106.), which led to a tribute to Vietnam at the Fox Theater in Detroit.

All of these events centered around food and people, food being the catalyst to bring people together. The recipes in this section are those that have made their way around the world with me—kind of old traveling buddies.

The Michigan Lunch in Paris was a celebration of the inauguration of the new American Ambassador to France, Mr. J.P. Curley. The luncheon was held at his private residence in Paris, a 20-room mansion staffed by butlers, chauffeurs, chefs, and

security. I handpicked a team of 16 staff members from Les Auteurs and we set off together for France. The year was 1989.

My intention was to prepare an all-Michigan luncheon with only ingredients from Michigan, including the wines served. A total of 2,900 pounds of food, wine, and equipment was shipped by special governmental pouch. The lunch, for 120 dignitaries and politicians, did Michigan proud.

The Michigan Dinner in China...Please allow me to quote Albert Einstein "In the midst of all difficulty lies opportunity." And we certainly were presented with a situation in Shanghai to transform difficulty into opportunity.

The plan was simple. Michigan was in the process of opening a new trade office in Shanghai. What better opportunity to showcase Michigan foods and cooking styles than an event of this nature? With the blessing and support of the Wisne family, who owned Forte Restaurant in Birmingham, Michigan, and the support of local business sponsorship, I set off to China in 1997 with Donna Brown, Ralph Moccochi, Matias, food writer Ruth Mossak Johnson and a cargo of food. Of course there had been months of preparation for this 120-person dinner, including a three-day trip to Shanghai for preliminary planning.

We finally arrived in Shanghai. We were primed for this event. Then, it happened. All of the food, so carefully selected to represent Michigan, never made it through customs. We had to go shopping—quickly. With a great deal of help from the hotel chef we were able to recreate a Michigan-inspired dinner.

Above: Donna Brown, Ralph Moccochi and I enjoyed every minute of our visit to Shanghi.

Far Left: Last minute shopping for dinner. I had to learn to balance the basket.

Left: I was having so much fun...until the snake bit me.

Seared Duck Breast with Molasses and Blackberry Sauce | Serves 4

3 tablespoons butter
1 carrot, finely diced
1 stalk of celery, finely diced
1 cup shiitake mushrooms, finely diced
1 cup fresh or frozen blackberries
2 cups duck or veal stock
1 tablespoon molasses
1 teaspoon freshly ground black pepper
1 sprig fresh thyme, finely chopped
¼ cup olive oil
4-6 8-oz duck breasts, with skin
½ cabbage, sautéed
16 to 18 morels, sautéed

1. Preheat oven to 400.°

2. Melt 2 tablespoons of the butter in a saucepan over medium heat. Add the carrots, celery, and shiitake mushrooms and cook for 5 minutes, stirring constantly until softened.

3. Add the blackberries and cook for 3 minutes, stirring constantly. Add the veal stock, molasses, black pepper, and thyme. Bring to a low simmer and cook for 10 minutes.

4. Strain the sauce through a fine strainer, forcing the ingredients through as much as possible. Keep warm until ready to use.

5. Heat the olive oil in a sauté pan over medium heat. Place the duck breasts, skin side down, in the pan and cook until the skin is thoroughly browned. Turn the duck breasts over and brown on the other side. Transfer sauté pan to the oven and cook duck breasts until medium rare, approximately 8 to 10 minutes. Let rest for 10 minutes before slicing.

6. Return sauce to a simmer, do not boil, and whisk in the remaining tablespoon of butter.

7. Slice the duck breasts and arrange them in a fan shape on the serving plates over a bed of sautéed cabbage and morels. Drizzle sauce over the sliced duck and serve.

Wine Recommendation: Cabernet Sauvignon

Michigan Stuffed Morels with Smoked Whitefish Mousse

Serves 4

24 medium fresh morel mushrooms
1 cup skinless fresh whitefish, boned, and diced
1 cup smoked whitefish, boned, skinned, and diced
1 tablespoon flat leaf parsley, chopped
  salt and pepper to taste
2 cups heavy cream
¼ cup olive oil
¼ cup diced onions
1½ cups diced tomatoes
1 tablespoon horseradish sauce
1 cup tomato juice
1 teaspoon chopped dill
2 tablespoons butter
  dill and wilted spinach for garnish

1. Clean the morels and trim the stems.

2. Add the whitefish, parsley, salt and pepper to a food processor fitted with the steel blade, and pulse for 10 seconds. Slowly pour in 1 cup of the heavy cream and pulse until completely incorporated.

3. Spoon the whitefish mixture into a pastry bag fitted with a small tip and gently fill each morel. Place morels on a plate and store in the refrigerator until ready to cook.

4. Heat the olive oil in a saucepan over medium heat. Add the onions and tomatoes and cook until the onions are translucent, approximately 3 minutes. Add the horseradish and tomato juice and simmer for 2 to 3 minutes.

5. Add the remaining cup of heavy cream and cook for 2 minutes over medium heat. Strain the sauce through a fine sieve. Stir in the fresh dill. Keep warm until ready to use.

6. Melt the butter in a sauté pan over medium heat. Add morels to the pan, do not overcrowd, cooking in batches if necessary. Add enough water to the pan to cover the bottom; bring to a simmer. When the mousse is firm, the mushrooms are cooked.

7. Divide the mushrooms onto serving plates and ladle sauce around the mushrooms. Garnish with dill and wilted spinach.

Wine Recommendation: Sauvignon Blanc

Redskin Potato Salad with Bacon and Leeks

Serves 4

1½ lbs small redskin potatoes
½ lb bacon, diced small
½ cup plus 2 tablespoons olive oil
1 leek (white part only), rinsed thoroughly, finely chopped
3 teaspoons fresh dill, washed, patted dry, chopped
¼ cup apple cider vinegar
3 teaspoons whole grain mustard
3 teaspoons brown sugar
salt and pepper to taste

1. Place the potatoes in a large stockpot, cover with water, and bring to a boil. Reduce the heat and cook the potatoes about 20 minutes or until they are tender. Remove from heat, let cool, and cut the potatoes into quarters. Set aside.

2. Cook the bacon in a large sauté pan until crispy. Drain on paper toweling.

3. In a large sauté pan, heat 2 tablespoons of olive oil. Add the leeks and sauté until tender, about 3-5 minutes. Add cooked bacon to the leeks.

4. In a large bowl, combine the quartered potatoes, bacon-leek mixture and fresh dill. Toss gently to combine.

5. In a blender, combine the cider vinegar, mustard, and brown sugar. With the blender on, slowly add the remaining ½ cup olive oil in a steady stream to combine well.

6. Pour the dressing over the potatoes and toss gently to coat. Season with salt and pepper to taste. Serve warm.

Smoked Whitefish Wonton with Ginger-Soy Sauce

Makes 16 wontons

½   cup soy sauce

    juice from 1 orange (about ¼ cup)

1   teaspoon grated ginger

¼   cup rice wine vinegar

5   sprigs cilantro, chopped

1   8-oz skinless, boneless fresh pickerel, cut
    into chunks

1   4-oz skinless, boneless smoked whitefish, cut
    into chunks,
    salt and pepper to taste

1   cup heavy cream

16   wonton wrappers, egg roll size, (6x6)
    soba noodles and stir-fried vegetables for garnish

1. Place the bowl of a food processor in the refrigerator for at least 30 minutes to chill.

2. Meanwhile, to prepare the Ginger-Soy Sauce, combine the soy sauce, orange juice, ginger, and rice wine vinegar in a medium saucepan. Bring to a boil, reduce the heat, and stir in the cilantro. Set aside.

3. Remove the chilled work bowl from the refrigerator and fit it with the steel blade. Add the pickerel, smoked whitefish, salt and pepper to the bowl. Pulse 5 to 10 seconds. With the food processor on, slowly add the cream until the filling is firm but still soft—a mousse-like consistency.

4. Place about 2 tablespoons of the mousse filling in the center of each wonton wrapper.

5. Bring up the sides of each wonton and pinch the edges together at the top to form sack-like bundles.

6. Place the filled wontons in a steamer basket over boiling water. Cover the steamer and cook 12 to 15 minutes, working in batches if necessary.

7. Remove the cooked wontons from the steamer. Drizzle with the Ginger-Soy Sauce and garnish with Soba noodles and your favorite stir-fried vegetables. Serve immediately.

Potato Leek Soup   Serves 4

3   leeks, thoroughly washed and diced
1   stalk of celery, diced
2   tablespoons olive oil
3   Idaho potatoes, peeled and diced
½   cup dark beer
4   cups chicken stock
½   cup Gorgonzola cheese
1   tablespoon Italian flat leaf parsley, chopped
    salt and pepper to taste
4 to 6 slices of pancetta, thinly sliced
1   dill sprig

1. In a stockpot, sauté the leeks and celery in olive oil
    until tender, approximately 3 to 4 minutes. Add the
    potatoes, beer, and chicken stock; cook until tender,
    approximately 20 to 25 minutes.

2. Purée the potato-leek mixture in a blender, while slowly
    adding the Gorgonzola and parsley. Return mixture to
    stockpot and reheat, if necessary. Season to taste.

3. Preheat oven to 375.° Bake the pancetta until crispy,
    approximately 10 minutes.

4. Garnish Potato Leek Soup with pancetta and dill sprig.

Roasted Pork Loin with Damson Plum Glaze　　　　　Serves 4

American Spoons from Northern Michigan have always risen to the occasion when I was inspired to create a menu from Michigan. Their Damson Plum Preserves is ideal for this Roast Pork Loin glaze.

1	well-trimmed pork loin, approximately 4 to 5 lbs
	salt and pepper to taste
1	cup Damson Plum Preserves*
1	teaspoon ginger, chopped
1	teaspoon dry mustard mixed with 1 teaspoon water
1	tablespoon black pepper, roughly ground
½	cup cider vinegar
½	cup brown sugar
1	cup water
	swiss chard and roasted redskin potatoes for garnish

1. Preheat oven to 400.°

2. Beginning with plum preserves, add all ingredients to a 2-quart saucepan. Bring to a slow simmer and cook for 2 minutes. Remove from heat and allow to cool.

3. In a hot sauté pan, brown the pork loin an all sides. Season with salt and pepper. Transfer to an ovenproof pan. Ladle reserved glaze generously over pork loin.

4. Roast in oven until the internal temperature reaches 140.° (Check temperature with a meat thermometer inserted into center of pork loin.)

5. Allow to rest for 15 minutes before slicing. Garnish with braised swiss chard and roasted redskin potatoes.

Damson Plum Preserves can be ordered from American Spoons @ (231) 922-8111.

The Mediterranean

...Con Mucho Gusto

The Mediterranean will always be one of the places I am drawn back to. My first trip was to the south of France at the age of nineteen. I landed a job at the Hotel Loews in Monte Carlo. As a young man I learned a great deal more in Monte Carlo than simply how to prepare outstanding food; the casinos and beaches were big attractions for a young Midwesterner. Even now, I always return to the south of France and eat my way up and down the coast.

Eventually, my adventures took me a little further west, to the city of Montpelier. Recently, I had the opportunity to visit again and spend some time with Chefs Jacques and Laurent Pourcel, twin brothers. They co-own a 3-star restaurant and hotel in the city. Together we filmed a couple of remarkable television segments, later aired in the United States. Their style is fascinating.

I later made my way to Spain. The adventure began in Barcelona where I learned to prepare tapas, a selection of appetizers traditionally served in little open-air bistros. What an amazing way to eat—you can choose several different tapas from the selection for your dinner.

However, my primary goal was to discover the origin of paella. I found myself in the city of Valencia soon after leaving Barcelona. It is said that paella was first served in Valencia. I learned from the locals that it is prepared in a flat pan with 2″ sides; steel pans are best. The Spanish

feel that they make the best paella because they add a rich brown rice, grown specifically in Valencia, to the ingredients. My favorite type is made with squid ink; I ate it while sitting on a veranda with a good traveling friend, overlooking the ocean.

The time I spent in the Mediterranean provided me with the opportunity to learn about both the food and lifestyle of the various cultures in the area. The Mediterranean diet, as we all know, is one of the healthiest approaches to eating. Most of the diet is from seafood, legumes, fresh herbs, and vegetables. They do not consume a lot of meat and much of their fat intake is from olive oil, which is healthier than most other sources of fat.

As they say in the Mediterranean, "Eat with gusto!"

Opposie page, top: Jacques and Laurent Pourcel of Les Jardin de Sens.

Left: I found wonderful fresh almonds in the market.

Below: My travels took me to the rice fields in Valencia, the markets and in the wine warehouse of Fortant de France.

Tapenade with Roasted Red Pepper   Serves 4

1   cup assorted olives, pitted*
2   tablespoons capers, rinsed
2   small cloves garlic, minced
6   anchovies, minced
     juice of 1 lemon
6   tablespoons olive oil
1   roasted red pepper, thinly sliced
     baguette slices, toasted

1. Place the olives, capers, garlic, anchovies, and lemon
    juice in a food processor, fitted with the metal blade,
    and pulse until well blended. With the processor still
    running add the olive oil in a steady stream until
    incorporated. Tapenade should be of a spreadable
    consistency.

2. Place the Tapenade mixture in an airtight container
    and refrigerate until ready to use.

3. When ready to serve, spread a little Tapenade on a
    slice of baguette and top with a slice of roasted red
    pepper.

I recommend Nicoise, Calamata, or Alfoso

Tuna Nicoise Salad with Mustard Vinaigrette   Serves 4

When I was in the Mediterranean, Tuna Nicoise Salad was a daily lunch item, eaten while sitting in the warm sun at a beach or in a cafe. Canned tuna is really and truly the best choice for this recipe. Use the highest quality canned tuna you can find; packed in olive oil—trust me, this is the way they do it in the Mediterranean. The name Nicoise comes from the name of the olives used in the salad.

2	heads Boston lettuce, cleaned and dried
4	6-oz cans tuna packed in olive oil, drained
2	cups fresh green or yellow wax beans, cleaned and blanched
1	cup Nicoise olives
8	hard-boiled eggs, halved
8	small vine-ripened tomatoes, quartered
8	anchovies
½	cup flat leaf parsley
½	cup small capers, rinsed and drained
	Mustard Vinaigrette
	chives, for garnish

Divide the lettuce onto serving plates. Place a serving of tuna in the center of the lettuce on each plate. Arrange the green beans, olives, eggs, tomatoes and anchovies decoratively around the tuna. Sprinkle with chopped parsley and capers. Drizzle with Mustard Vinaigrette. Garnish with chives.

Mustard Vinaigrette

1	cup olive oil
¼	cup Balsamic vinegar
¼	cup red wine vinegar
1	teaspoon garlic, chopped
1	tablespoon fresh basil, chopped
1	tablespoon Dijon mustard

Place all ingredients in a blender and process until thoroughly combined.

Wine Recommendation: Sauvignon Blanc

Olives with Harissa and Cilantro

Makes enough for 4 nibblers

This is such an easy dish but is always a favorite. Its uniqueness stems from two things. First, you eat the olives warm and second, because it calls for harissa—a North African roasted pepper paste with oil and seasonings. This recipe calls for three kinds of olives. It's best to buy them fresh at a Middle Eastern specialty market, which by the way, is where you'll find the harissa.

- ½ cup olive oil
- 1 cup Calamata olives
- 1 cup green olives
- 1 cup Nicoise olives
- 1 teaspoon garlic, chopped
- 1 teaspoon harissa*
- ½ cup chopped fresh cilantro

Heat the olive oil and olives in a large nonstick sauté pan over medium heat. Add the garlic and sauté for one minute. Stir in the harissa and cilantro. Serve warm.

Harissa is very hot; start with a little and add more if you want more heat!

Fresh Mozzarella, Tomato and Onion Salad

Serves 4

Summer brings so many wonderful items from the garden! This is a celebration lunch dish or a first course for dinner. You can't lose with vine-ripened tomatoes and fresh basil. Note: Add a can of tuna for another delectable meal.

- 2 bunches of arugula, washed and patted dry
- 4 6-oz balls of fresh mozzarella, sliced
- 4 medium vine-ripened tomatoes, sliced
- 8 leaves of fresh basil
- 4 large leaves radicchio, julienned
   freshly ground black pepper to taste
   Balsamic Vinaigrette

Divide the arugula onto serving plates. Add alternate slices of mozzarella, tomatoes, and basil leaves. Scatter the julienned radicchio around each salad. Grind black pepper over each serving and drizzle with Balsamic Vinaigrette.

Balsamic Vinaigrette

- 1 cup olive oil
- ½ cup Balsamic vinegar
- 1 tablespoon water
- 1 tablespoon Dijon mustard
- 1 clove garlic, finely chopped
   salt and pepper to taste
- 1 tablespoon dark opal basil
- 1 teaspoon chives

Place all ingredients in a blender. Process at high speed until thoroughly combined.

Bouillabaisse

There's an ongoing debate about whether or not a true Bouillabaisse can be made outside of the Marseille region of France. The debate originates with the ingredients used in a true French Bouillabaisse. It is said that only the red gunard fish and the scorpion fish can be used in a true Bouillabaisse. Both fish are native to that region in France; hence they are used in the Bouillabaisse. When you make this dish just call it Fisherman's Soup and use the following ingredients or your favorite seafood.

1 cup olive oil
6 cloves garlic, chopped
3 leeks, white part only, diced
1 large white onion, diced
4 ripe tomatoes
1 10-oz can diced tomatoes
1 whole lobster, cut into pieces
1 teaspoon dried fennel
1 teaspoon dried thyme
1 teaspoon dried basil
½ teaspoon fresh flat leaf parsley
½ teaspoon cayenne pepper
1 teaspoon saffron, soaked in ½ cup white wine
½ lb mussels
½ lb clams
1 cup white wine
4 lbs assorted fish, boned and diced*
2 tablespoons tomato paste
1 lb king crab legs
2 quarts canned clam stock
   fresh basil, cut into ribbons, for garnish

1. Heat the olive oil in a large stockpot over medium heat. Add garlic, leeks, and onion and cook for 2 minutes, stirring continually. Add the tomatoes and lobster; cook for three minutes. Add the herbs, saffron/wine liquid, mussels, and clams and cook for 3 minutes, continuing to stir. Add the white wine and cook for 2 additional minutes.

2. Add the fish, tomato paste, crab legs, and clam stock and cook on a low simmer for 15 minutes.

3. Serve with ribbons of basil.

* Red Snapper, Ocean Catfish, or Halibut

Wine Recommendation: Chardonnay

Lobster Maxim

Serves 4

I first enjoyed this dish at the Chanticleer Restaurant in the Negresso Hotel in Nice, France. It is one of the most remarkable places I have ever eaten. This dish is the splendid creation of its Chef, Jacques Maxima.

3	carrots, unpeeled and blanched*
1	2-lb whole lobster, boiled, meat removed and diced
1	leek, white part only, cleaned, blanched and diced
1	cup cooked brown lentils
1	rib celery, diced and sautéed in olive oil
1	tablespoon chopped fresh dill
¾	cup olive oil
½	cup red wine vinegar
	salt and pepper to taste
2	cups mixed greens
1	English cucumber, peeled and thinly sliced
	Tomato Vinaigrette
	chives, dill sprigs and celery leaves for garnish

1. To prepare the Lobster Maxim, dice one of the carrots and place in a large bowl. Add the lobster, leek, lentils, celery, and fresh dill and mix well. Reserve meat from lobster claws for garnish.

2. In a separate bowl, whisk together the olive oil, vinegar, and salt and pepper and toss with the lobster mixture.

3. Slice the remaining two carrots lengthwise as thin as possible and reserve.

4. Using a 2˝ pastry ring or a small souffle dish lined with plastic wrap, arrange carrot slices inside. Pour Lobster Maxim over carrots.

5. Invert pastry ring on serving plate. Ladel Tomato vinaigrette over Lobster Maxim. Wrap with chives. Arrange cucumbers on plate. Garnish with fresh dill celery leaves and lobster claws.

*Carrots are cooked when a toothpick can be gently inserted into carrot. Cool and peel.

Tomato Vinaigrette

	reserved tomato liquid from **Tomato Concasse**
¼	cup red wine vinegar
½	cup olive oil
	salt and pepper to taste

In a small bowl, whisk together the tomato liquid, vinegar, olive oil, and salt and pepper. Refrigerate until ready to serve.

Tomato Concasse

1	lb Roma tomatoes, blanched, skinned, and diced
1½	tablespoons olive oil

In a medium saucepan, sauté diced tomatoes in olive oil. Strain the tomatoes through a fine sieve set over a bowl. Reserve liquid.

 *Wine Recommendation: White Burgundy*

Valencia Paella

Serves 4

Spain is a majestic place to visit. I was fortunate to have the opportunity to spend several weeks there learning about the food and culture. Paella was created in the city of Valencia. You'll need a paella pan to prepare it. Once you've learn how to prepare it you can create your own variations of this very simple dish.

12	oz veal shoulder, cut into ½″ cubes
4	boneless, skinless chicken thighs
1	cup olive oil
8	large shrimp, peeled and deveined, tails intact
8	oz firm fish such as tilapia, catfish, or sea bass, cut into ½″ cubes
12	mussels
12	littleneck clams
2	medium tomatoes, diced
1	red pepper, diced
1	16-oz can diced tomatoes
2	small carrots, diced
1	small white onion, diced
1	cup Arborio rice
2	teaspoons oregano
2	teaspoons garlic cloves, finely chopped
	salt and pepper to taste
2	cups water

1. Preheat oven to 375.°

2. Brown the veal in a nonstick pan and set aside. Repeat with chicken.

3. Heat the olive oil in a paella pan over medium-high heat, and add the shrimp, fish, mussels, and clams; sauté 3 minutes while stirring continually.

4. Add the diced tomato, red pepper, canned tomatoes, carrots, onion, rice, oregano, and garlic. Season with salt and pepper. Cook for 3 to 5 minutes, then stir in water. Mix well.

5. Place the paella pan in the oven and bake for 20 minutes. The paella is done when the rice is cooked. If the rice is dry but not cooked, pour an additional ½ cup water over the top.

Wine Recommendation: Sangria

Spicy Morrocan Salmon with Calamata Mashed Potatoes   Serves 4

½ cup whole coriander
½ cup cumin seeds
½ cup fennel seeds
1 teaspoon whole allspice
1 teaspoon whole cloves
4 6-oz salmon filets
4 tablespoons olive oil
Spicy Tomato Sauce
Calamata Mashed Potatoes
salt and pepper to taste

1. Preheat oven to 400.°

2. Grind each spice separately in a coffee grinder. Mix together in a small bowl.

3. Place spice mixture on a dinner plate and dredge one side of each piece of salmon in mixture, pressing down gently to coat well.

4. Heat 2 tablespoons of the olive oil in a large sauté pan over medium heat. Place the salmon filets, spice side down, in the pan. Season with salt and pepper. Brown lightly on each side, approximately 2 minutes per side.

5. Coat an ovenware pan, large enough to hold the filets, with the remaining olive oil. Add the filets to the pan and place in the oven. Bake until salmon can be gently flaked or feels firm to the touch, approximately 15 minutes. Serve with Spicy Tomato Sauce and Calamata Mashed Potatoes.

My favorite presentation of this dish includes fresh asparagus and yellow wax beans.

❧ *Wine Recommendation: Chardonnay*

Spicy Tomato Sauce

1 tablespoon olive oil
1 small red onion, chopped
1 tablespoon garlic, minced
1 cup diced tomatoes
1 cup tomato juice
½ cup vegetable stock
1 tablespoon fresh parsley, chopped
1 tablespoon fresh cilantro, chopped
½ teaspoon ground cumin
½ teaspoon ground fennel
½ teaspoon paprika
½ teaspoon ground celery seed
1½ tablespoons salt and pepper

1. Place the olive oil in a large stainless stockpot, and sauté the onion over medium heat until softened, approximately 3 to 4 minutes. Add the garlic and cook, stirring, for 1 minute.

2. Add the tomatoes, tomato juice, and vegetable stock and cook at a simmer for 15 minutes. Stir in the herbs and spices and season with salt and pepper. Keep warm.

Calamata Mashed Potatoes

6 Idaho potatoes
½ cup Calamata olives, pitted and finely chopped
½ cup butter (1 stick)
½ cup heavy cream
salt and pepper to taste

Peel the potatoes, cut into pieces, and boil in a large pot of salted water until tender. Drain well and place in the bowl of an electric mixer. Using the wire whisk attachment, whip the potatoes; add the chopped olives. Add the butter and cream while continuing to whip. Salt and pepper to taste.

Vietnam

Truly a Great Adventure

Vietnam definitely ranks high on my list of "Most Adventurous Places to Visit." My excursion to Vietnam, which centered around a biking trip from Hanoi to Hoi-An, was one of my greatest adventures. I traveled with a group from "Cycle the World," an Oregon bicycle tour outfit that included several Vietnam Vets. Our trip was the first time these men had returned since fighting on that soil during the Vietnam War. They added a dimension to this trip that I had never experienced in my life.

We started from Hanoi, the oldest capital city in Southeast Asia. We were met by Chef Didier, Executive Chef of the five star Metropole Hotel in Hanoi. He served as our guide to the flavors, sights, and sounds of this fascinating city. At the market place I sipped snake wine and nibbled at thousand-year-old eggs! This cuisine is deeply rooted in the rich history of Vietnam and draws from Chinese and French influences. It's unbelievable. From Hanoi, we traveled down the coast to Hoi-an and China Beach, making friends and absorbing the culture and landscape of this exquisite country.

During our tour, we filmed a documentary about Vietnam which premiered at the Fox Theater in Detroit and was later nominated for a local Emmy award.

Far right: My buddy and cameraman, Kevin Hewitt.

Above: Invitation and tickets to the Vietnam Documentary at the Fox Theater in Detroit.

Left: I enjoyed bicycling to the market.

Below: Kevin Hewitt and I in Hue.

Vietnamese Banana Flower Salad   Serves 6

This fascinating salad uses an actual flower from the banana tree as well as a green papaya. I learned how to prepare this alongside Chef Didier of the Metropole Hotel in Hanoi. You can locate banana flowers in Oriental or Vietnamese markets. If you can't find fresh banana flowers you can substitute the canned variety.

1   cup water
    juice of one lemon
1   fresh banana flower, sliced into thin ribbons
2   cups daikon radish, finely julienned
1   cup bean sprouts, rinsed
1   green papaya, peeled and julienned
1   small red chili, chopped
½   cup chopped cilantro
½   cup unsalted peanuts, chopped
¾   cup bottled Vietnamese sweet and sour sauce
1   tablespoon bottled fish sauce
¼   cup light soy sauce
1   clove garlic, chopped
1   teaspoon chopped ginger

1. Squeeze the juice from the lemon into a small bowl of water. Soak the ribbons of banana flower in lemon water for 20 minutes, drain.

2. In a large bowl mix together the banana flower, daikon radish, bean sprouts, papaya, chili, cilantro, and peanuts.

3. In a separate small bowl, whisk together the sweet and sour sauce, fish sauce, soy sauce, garlic, and ginger.

4. Pour the sauce over the banana flower mixture and toss gently to coat evenly. Refrigerate the salad for one hour.

5. Garnish with roasted, chopped, unsalted peanuts and flower petals.

Pumpkin Branches with Garlic   Serves 4

Chef Didier and I filmed several TV segments while I was in his kitchen. One featured this recipe for sautéed Pumpkin Branches. It's a very simple idea that utilizes the long stems that run from the vine to the pumpkin. They are really very good and healthy! Did you know that you can also eat the leaves of the plant? They are similar to spinach.

¼   cup olive oil
4   cloves garlic, roughly chopped
2   pumpkin stems with leaves intact, about 2
        feet in length, roughly chopped
    salt and pepper to taste

Heat the olive oil in a large nonstick sauté pan over medium heat. Add the garlic and cook for a few minutes, taking care not to burn the garlic. Add the pumpkin stems and cook for 1 or 2 minutes while tossing gently to coat. Season with salt and pepper.

Vietnamese Steamed Pickerel

Serves 2

When I was in Hanoi I had this dish prepared with snake fish. They are abundant in the local river.

2	8-oz filets of pickerel*
1	small leek, cleaned and julienned
1	small carrot, julienned
1	stalk of celery, julienned
6	shiitake mushrooms, julienned
1	red chili, julienned
1	teaspoon tumeric
	12-oz fish stock
	salt and pepper to taste
¼	cup cilantro, chopped

1. Place each of the fish filets on a 10˝ plate and season with salt and pepper to taste. Distribute the julienned vegetables over the fish, sprinkle with the tumeric, and pour the fish stock over all.

2. Set each plate in a hot steamer and steam for 10 to 15 minutes or until the fish flakes when tested with a fork. Garnish with chopped cilantro.

Note: If you don't have a steamer, you can make one by adding approximately 2˝ of water to the bottom of an ovenproof pan. Place plates in pan and cover with foil. Cut several small slits in the foil to allow the steam to escape.

* If available, substitute snake fish for pickerel.

Chicken with Famie's Green Curry Paste

Serves 4

This recipe is, by far, my favorite Vietnamese dish. It is extremely easy to make. You'll find that it combines the subtle flavors of coconut milk while at the same time imparts a pleasant hint of curry. There are quite a few varieties of curry available from Southeast Asian stores, but try mine; I think you'll like it.

4	6-oz boneless breasts of chicken
2	tablespoons olive oil
1	medium-size onion, diced
1	8-oz package dried shiitake mushrooms, soaked in warm water, drained and quartered
2	pieces fresh bamboo (carrot size), diced, rinsed, and cut into bite-size pieces
1	red bell pepper, diced
2	tablespoons **Famie's Green Curry Paste**
1	8-oz can coconut milk
1	16-oz can chicken stock
1	teaspoon cornstarch
	salt and pepper to taste
1	small bunch cilantro

1. Sauté chicken breasts in a hot pan until they are 80% cooked, approximately 15 minutes. Dice and set aside.

2. Heat the olive oil in a large saucepan. Add the onions, shiitake mushrooms, bamboo, and pepper and cook until softened, approximately 3 to 4 minutes. Add curry paste and continue to cook for 3 minutes over medium heat.

3. Add the coconut milk, chicken stock and the reserved chicken and simmer for 10 minutes, stirring occasionally. Briskly stir in the cornstarch, if necessary, to thicken. Season to taste with salt and pepper. Just prior to serving, gently stir in the cilantro.

Delicious with fluffy white rice.

Famie's Green Curry Paste

2	oz coriander seeds
1	hefty pinch black mustard seeds
2	small green hot chiles, roasted and peeled
2	garlic cloves, roughly chopped
1½	oz fresh ginger, chopped
2	cups cilantro, stemmed and roughly chopped
1	teaspoon ground turmeric
1	tablespoon chopped lemongrass
¼	cup white vinegar
1	cup olive oil
1	tablespoon kosher salt

1. In a nonstick pan, toast the coriander seeds until they are crunchy. Grind in a coffee grinder.

2. Add the coriander seeds to a blender along with the black mustard seeds, chiles, garlic, ginger, cilantro, turmeric, lemongrass, and vinegar. Blend until smooth.

3. Sauté paste mixture and olive oil in a non stick pan. Do not burn; when the oil starts to separate from the paste, it is done.

4. Add the kosher salt and stir well. This will help preserve it. When the curry paste is cool, place in a glass jar and keep refrigerated.

One of the nicest things about curry paste is that it keeps well in the refrigerator. Watch out though, the flavor intensifies with age.

Stir-Fried Chicken with Green Papaya, Mango, and Peanuts

Serves 4

Here is a great little technique I use to tenderize chicken. Fry the diced chicken for three minutes in hot peanut oil before using in a stir-fry. This recipe is very quick and easy and will allow you to experience the adventure of the Vietnamese cuisine without ever leaving home!

4½	cups peanut oil
4	boneless breasts of chicken, diced
1	red chili pepper, with seeds, diced
1	tablespoon garlic, chopped
4	scallions, chopped
½	cup pea pods
½	cup green papaya, peeled and julienned
1	teaspoon grated ginger
1	cup chopped tomatoes
½	cup diced fresh ripe mango
	juice of two limes
1	tablespoon sugar
3	tablespoons fish sauce
½	cup roasted, unsalted peanuts
1	red bell pepper, julienned
8	small shiitake mushrooms, quartered
½	cup cilantro, roughly chopped

1. Heat 4 cups of the peanut oil to 350.° Fry the diced chicken in the peanut oil for 2 to 3 minutes. Set aside.

2. Heat the remaining peanut oil in a wok over medium-high heat. Add the chili pepper, garlic, scallions, pea pods, and papaya; stir-fry for 2 minutes. Add the reserved chicken, ginger, tomatoes, and mango.

3. Stir in the lime juice, sugar, fish sauce, peanuts, red bell pepper, and shiitake mushrooms. Add the cilantro; stir. Serve immediately.

Fresh Fish Spring Rolls   Makes 12 rolls

I had this dish in a little restaurant in Hue, (pronounced WAY). A whole snapper was fried then brought to the table where the waitperson took the fish off of the bones and wrapped it in individual rolls. I have altered the recipe so that you don't have to fry a whole fish.

1   10-oz halibut filet
½   cup olive oil
    salt and pepper to taste
¼   cup bottled Vietnamese fish sauce
1   cup bottled Sweet and Sour Vietnamese Sauce
12 sheets 6˝ rice paper
2   cups fresh bean sprouts
1   cup cilantro, roughly chopped
    loose green tea, for garnish

1. Preheat oven to 400.°

2. Place the halibut filets on a sheet pan or sturdy cookie sheet, rub with olive oil, and season with salt and pepper. Place in oven and bake until the fish flakes, approximately 12 to 15 minutes. Remove from oven. Gently flake fish into a serving bowl.

3. In a separate small bowl, mix fish sauce with sweet and sour sauce. Set aside.

4. Dip the rice paper into warm water and allow to soak for several minutes to soften. Select a piece of rice paper, lay on a flat surface, and place a small amount of fish in the center. Add a few bean sprouts and cilantro. Top with a spoonful of the fish sauce mixture, and roll up. Serve on platter sprinkled with green tea leaves. Now, prepare yourself for a treat!

Sugarcane Steamed Fish

Serves 2

Sugarcane is abundant in Southeast Asia. It is used in a variety of ways, from juice drinks to simply chewing on it. This recipe not only relies on the use of sugarcane in the preparation of the dish, it also creates a dramatic presentation. The whole meal is cooked on a plate steamed in your oven. You can use a bamboo steamer if you wish.

2   5″ pieces sugarcane
2   8-oz pieces of a firm fleshed fish*
Marinade
Garnish

1. Preheat oven to 400.°

2. With a sharp knife, slice the sugarcane lengthwise into 3 long slices. Cut each slice into 3 or 4 strips, depending on their thickness. Set aside.

3. Place the fish filets in a dish and cover with marinade. Marinate for 20 minutes.

4. Select an ovenproof dish, appropriate for serving, with sides high enough to retain the marinade while steaming. Arrange the sugarcane lattice-style on the dish. Lay the fish on the sugarcane. Sprinkle garnishes on fish. Pour approximately ½″ of marinade on the fish and garnish. Add a teaspoon or two of water.

5. Cover and place in oven for 15 minutes or longer, depending on the thickness of the fish. Fish will flake easily with a fork when done. Serve immediately.

* Tilapia, sea bass, pompano, or mackerel

Marinade

1   cup rice wine vinegar
1   teaspoon garlic, chopped
1   teaspoon ginger, chopped
½   cup soy sauce
¼   cup sesame oil
½   cup fish sauce
¼   cup oyster sauce
    zest from 1 lemon

Beginning with rice wine vinegar, mix all remaining ingredients for marinade together in a bowl. Transfer to blender and pulse for approximately 20 seconds.

Garnish

1   scallion, cut on bias
2   red chiles, sliced on diagonal into medium-sized pieces
1   cup straw mushrooms
3   Chinese long beans
8   baby corn
2   sprigs of cilantro

Vietnamese Shrimp & Scallop Salad   Serves 4

This is a great way to transform an ordinary BBQ into a Southeast Asian affair. It's simple to prepare and the lemongrass skewers are a wonderful conversation starter.

16   large Gulf shrimp, peeled & deveined
16   Sea scallops
8   pieces lemongrass, cut in 4˝ pieces, trimmed
     to form a point on one end
½   cup Hoisin sauce
½   tablespoon ginger, peeled & minced
½   tablespoon garlic, minced
1   tablespoon cilantro, chopped
½   cup extra virgin olive oil
½   cup Soy Ginger Marinade*

Salad

½   head green cabbage, shredded
1   red pepper, julienne
1   yellow pepper, julienne
½   red onion, julienne
½   cup rice wine vinegar
2   tablespoons sesame seeds, toasted
½   cup extra virgin olive oil
½   cup unsalted peanuts, toasted & chopped

1. Thread 2 shrimp and 2 scallops alternately on pieces of lemon grass.

2. Combine Hoisin sauce, ginger, garlic, cilantro, olive oil and Soy Ginger Marinade in a small bowl; whisk until ingredients are well blended. Transfer to a 13x9x2˝ dish. Place lemongrass skewers in dish and marinate for 1 hour, turning after 30 minutes.

3. While the shrimp and scallops are marinating mix all salad ingredients. Refrigerate until ready to serve.

4. Remove shrimp and scallops from marinade and grill or broil until done, approximately 3 to 4 minutes.

5. Divide salad equally among individual plates. Serve shrimp and scallops, on their skewers, over salad.

Soy Ginger Marinade is available through Whole Foods Markets: (512) 477-5566

Adventures in Desserts
A Lesson in Decadence

I never really appreciated pastries until I had the chance to work in two places. The first was in New York at the Plaza Hotel and the second, at Bloomingdales for Chef Michael Geurard's Gourmet-To-Go market. It was here that I had the opportunity to develop a passion for pastries and desserts. Two very different worlds. At the Geurard market, I had to be at work at 8:00 a.m. I spent the majority of the day working in a walk-in cooler preparing all of the puff pastry. At the Plaza, I would arrive at work at 5:00 p.m. and work until 1:00 a.m. I prepared 2,000 mini-eclairs, 400 rice puddings, and 1,500 petit fours, daily.

Over the years, I've learned to become my best mentor on desserts. My style is French with a flair for simplicity. Since then I have had the opportunity to work with several outstanding pastry chefs and bakers. They have taught me many techniques, and I will be forever grateful.

Here are some recipes for my favorite desserts that I've collected through the years.

Sweet Potato Bread Pudding

Serves 8

3 large sweet potatoes, baked, peeled and mashed
7 slices good quality French bread, diced
½ cup dried Traverse City cherries, diced
3 eggs
2 egg yolks
2 cups heavy cream
½ teaspoon cinnamon
¼ teaspoon nutmeg
2 tablespoons brown sugar
Rum Raisin Sauce
cinnamon and sugar mixture

1. Preheat oven to 350.°

2. In a large bowl, blend the sweet potatoes with the diced bread and dried cherries. In another bowl mix the eggs, heavy cream, cinnamon, nutmeg and brown sugar together. Stir the egg mixture into the potato mixture until well blended.

3. Pour the batter into buttered 9x5x3″ loaf pan, cover with parchment paper and bake in a water bath* for 25 to 30 minutes, or until a toothpick inserted in the center is clean. Remove from oven and let cool.

4. Unmold onto serving dish, drizzle with Rum Raisin Sauce; dust with cinnamon sugar blend.

To create a water bath, place the loaf pan in an ovenproof 13x 9″ pan filled with approximately 1½″ of water.

Rum Raisin Sauce

¼ cup dark raisins
3 oz rum
1 cup milk
¼ cup heavy whipping cream
1 vanilla bean split and scraped of seeds **or** 1 teaspoon vanilla extract
4 large egg yolks
¼ cup sugar

1. In a small saucepan, boil raisins and rum until liquid is reduced to approximately 1 ounce. Set aside.

2. In the top half of a double boiler, bring the milk, cream and vanilla to a boil, stirring constantly. Reduce the heat and simmer for 3-4 minutes.

3. In a medium bowl, whisk together the egg yolks and sugar. Stir ¼ cup of the warm milk mixture into the egg mixture. Then, pour the entire egg mixture into the double boiler mixture. Add rum raisin liquid. Mix thoroughly over medium to low heat for 4 minutes, stirring constantly until the mixture lightly coats the back of a wooden spoon.

4. Remove the sauce from the heat and strain it into a medium bowl, using a mesh strainer to remove any particles of cooked egg.

 *Serve with Champagne*

Poached Late Summer Harvest Fruits

Serves 4

This is, by far, one of my favorite desserts. I became fond of poached fruits during my trips to France. The French take a creative approach to poaching fruits. This is my version with a secret* ingredient that makes all the difference. See if you can guess what it is!

3	cups sugar
2	cups fresh black cherries
1	tablespoon whole black peppercorns
1	teaspoon cloves
3	cinnamon sticks
1	red Bartlett pear
1	nectarine
2	peaches
2	oranges, peeled and sectioned
2	thick slices of fresh pineapple
2	cups heavy cream

1. In a large saucepan, heat sugar in 6 cups of water until simmering. Add 1 cup of cherries to the water along with the spices; simmer for 10 minutes. Add the pear, nectarine, peaches, pineapple, and remaining cherries, and simmer for 10 minutes. Make certain that mixture does not boil.

2. Test the fruit for doneness with a sharp paring knife. Remove the fruit from the poaching liquid while it is still a little firm. Reserve liquid.

3. Place the poached fruit in a shallow bowl and refrigerate. Do not place fruit on top of other fruit. Add oranges. Pour ¾ of the poaching liquid over the fruit. Refrigerate.

4. Pour remaining poaching liquid into a small saucepan and boil until reduced by half. Refrigerate until cold.

5. When ready to serve, slice the poached fruit and arrange on a serving platter.

6. In large mixing bowl, whip the heavy cream to soft peaks. Fold in the refrigerated poaching liquid. Spoon over fruits.

*My secret ingredient is black peppercorns.

Cup of Mud

Serves 4

This is a simple fun dessert loved by one and all. Serve it in an enamel camping cup like we did at Durango and listen to everyone shout "Yee Ha!"

4	cups **Chocolate Mousse**
1	cup ground Oreo® cookies

1. Remove the cream filling from the Oreos and grind the chocolate cookies in a food processor.

2. Fill serving cups with Chocolate Mousse to a half inch from the top.

3. Top with ground Oreo cookies and store in the refrigerator for at least 30 minutes before serving.

Chocolate Mousse

1	15-oz semisweet chocolate
1	lb unsalted butter
8	egg yolks
1	cup sugar
8	egg whites

1. Melt chocolate and butter over a double boiler. Remove from heat.

2. In a separate bowl, beat egg yolks and ½ cup sugar until smooth and doubled in volume. Add yolk mixture to the melted chocolate; stir to blend.

3. In another bowl, beat whites until stiff; add remaining sugar. Fold gently into chocolate mixture. Refrigerate for 2 hours.

Chocolate Sticks

½	cup melted semi-sweet chocolate
3	large plastic drinking straws
	parchment paper
	bamboo skewer

1. Roll a sheet of parchment paper into a cone shape and fill with the melted chocolate. Fill the straws by holding your finger over one end and squeezing the chocolate from the parchment paper cone into the other end of the straw. Place the chocolate-filled straws in the refrigerator until hardened, approximately 20 minutes.

2. To remove the chocolate straws, use a bamboo skewer to gently push the chocolate from the straw. Break chocolate straw into pieces and place them on top of your Cup of Mud.

Gourmet Cowboy S'Mores   Serves 2

In all my years in the restaurant business I've never seen any dessert take off and sell the way this one did. You can make it in your own kitchen. What's the secret? Try them for yourself and see if you don't agree that it's the toasted hazelnuts.

1   cup water
¼   cup + 1 tablespoon granulated sugar
½   cup hazelnuts, chopped
3   egg whites
3   large graham crackers, broken in half
2   1.5-oz. chocolate bars
1   bag of large marshmallows
4   large strawberries, sliced

1. Preheat oven to 350.°

2. To make meringue: In a small bowl, beat the egg whites until stiff. Gradually beat in 1 tablespoon of sugar. Set aside for later use.

3. Sprinkle hazelnuts evenly on a sheet tray. Bake in oven for 7 to 10 minutes, or until toasted. Remove from oven.

4. In a small saucepan, boil remaining sugar and water until sugar begins to caramelize. It will become amber in color. Remove from stove and immediately set in a bowl of ice water, taking care not to get any cold water in the sugar mixture.

5. Using toothpicks with frills on one end, stick the bare end of the toothpick into roasted hazelnuts. Dip each one into the caramelized sugar mixture to coat. Insert the frilled end of the toothpick into a piece of stryofoam. Invert the styrofoam so that the hazelnuts hang upside down to dry. (Lay a piece of parchment paper under the hazelnuts to catch any drips.)

6. Lay 1 graham cracker on each of 2 plates. Top with marshmallows. Break pieces of the chocolate bar and place on top of marshmallows. Layer with another graham cracker, marshmallows, and chocolate. Gently place another graham cracker on the top of S'Mores.

7. Top with meringue. Holding a small butane torch approximately 6˝ away from S'Mores, carefully toast until marshmallows and meringue are brown and chocolate melts. An alternate method would be to use a broiler to brown meringue and melt chocolate.

8. Top with roasted hazelnuts and garnish with strawberries.

Oven Baked Apple Pecan Pancake

Serves 2 to 3

3   eggs
½   cup milk
¾   cup pancake mix
⅓   cup sugar
2   large tart cooking apples, peeled, cored & sliced
¼   cup chopped pecans
1   teaspoon cinnamon
    maple or apple-cinnamon syrup

1. Preheat oven to 450.°

2. Spray a 9″ glass pie dish with nonstick cooking spray; set aside.

3. In a medium bowl, beat eggs. Add milk, pancake mix and 1 teaspoon of sugar; mix thoroughly with a wire whisk. Set aside.

4. Place apple slices in pie dish and cover tightly with plastic wrap. Microwave on high for 5 to 6 minutes, or until apples are tender. Sprinkle pecans over apples; pour reserved batter over all.

5. Combine remaining sugar with cinnamon and sprinkle over batter.

6. Cover with foil and bake for 10 to 12 minutes, or until pancake is set.

7. Cut in wedges and drizzle with maple syrup or apple-cinnamon syrup.

Autumn Apple Bake

Serves 4

Autumn is my favorite time of the year. During this season, I become very stimulated by all of the fruits and vegetables that are available during the harvest. Apples have to be one of the most versatile fruits for desserts. Here's one of my favorite apple desserts.

4	Granny Smith apples
½	cup raisins, chopped fine
1	teaspoon ground cinnamon
2	cups pecans, chopped fine
1	cup brown sugar
½	cup dried cherries, chopped fine
½	cup butter
5	6x6 sheets puff pastry
2	egg whites for wash
	whipped cream for topping

1. Preheat oven to 400.°

2. Peel apples and completely hollow out the insides with a melon baller. Mix the remaining ingredients (with the exception of puff pastry, egg whites and whipped cream) together with a spoon or in a food processor. The mixture will have a paste appearance. Fill the apples from both ends with the mixture.

3. Wrap each apple in a sheet of puff pastry. With a small paring knife, cut the excess dough into shapes of leaves and decorate the tops of the apples with two leaves each.

4. Egg wash the puff pastry and bake until golden brown. Top with fresh whipped cream.

Serve with Champagne

Lady Fingers

5   eggs, separated
1½ cups + 2 tablespoons sugar
1   cup flour, sifted
    powdered sugar for dusting

1. Preheat oven to 375.°

2. On high speed with electric mixer beat egg yolks with
    1½ cups of sugar until doubled in volume, light and
    airy. Gently fold in flour. Set aside.

3. In a separate large bowl, beat egg whites with remaining
    sugar until soft peaks form. Fold yolk mixture into egg
    whites.

4. Immediately fill a pastry bag, using a plain tip with an
    opening approximately the size of a dime, with the egg
    mixture. Slowly pipe the mixture into 4˝ long strips on
    a cookie sheet. Bake in oven for 18 to 20 minutes.

5. Remove from oven and dust with powdered sugar.
    Rest at room temperature for 2 or 3 hours to dry out.

Michigan Apple and Cherry Cobbler

Serves 4

1½ lbs butter
1½ cups brown sugar
2   cinnamon sticks
8   Granny Smith apples, peeled, cored, and diced
1½ cups dried Michigan cherries
½   cup brandy
3   sheets pie dough or puff pastry
1   egg, beaten lightly for egg wash
     whipped cream for topping

1. Preheat oven to 400.°

2. In a sauté pan, melt butter with brown sugar and cinnamon. Stir in apples, cherries, and brandy. Cook over medium heat for 10 minutes, stirring occasionally until apples are soft. Remove the mixture from heat and cool to room temperature. This can be made a day ahead and refrigerated.

3. Fill 4 individual dishes or 1 9x9˝ glass or ceramic dish to the top with the apple mixture. Place pie dough on top of sure that you cover all of the mixture. Brush lightly with egg wash.

4. Bake in oven for 15-20 minutes or until the top is golden brown. Serve with fresh whipped cream.

Serve with Champagne.

Michigan Bread Pudding

Serves 6

3   tablespoons butter
2   Granny Smith apples, peeled, cored, and cubed
1   teaspoon vanilla
1½   teaspoons cinnamon
1   cup brown sugar
1   cup dried cherries (may substitute raisins)
½   teaspoon nutmeg
¼   teaspoon ground cloves
¾   cup Maker's Mark bourbon
2   cups heavy cream
3   eggs, lightly beaten
2   egg yolks, lightly beaten
6 to 7 cups small bread cubes, crusts removed*
     Michigan Maple Crème Anglaise

1. Preheat oven to 375.°

2. Butter an 8x8˝ baking pan with 1 tablespoon of the butter. Set aside.

3. In a large skillet, melt remaining butter, add the cubed apples, and sauté for about 3 minutes. Stir in the vanilla, cinnamon, brown sugar, dried cherries, nutmeg, cloves, and bourbon. Continue to cook until the apples are tender but hold their shape, approximately 5 to 7 minutes. Remove from heat and set aside to cool.

4. In a medium bowl, mix together the heavy cream, eggs, and egg yolks until well blended.

5. In a separate large bowl, mix together the bread cubes and sautéed apple mixture. Add half of the egg mixture and mix thoroughly. Spoon bread mixture into buttered loaf pan and pour the remaining custard over the top. Place the baking dish into a larger baking pan, about 2˝ deep. Pour warm water into the larger pan, to a depth about halfway up the outside of the baking dish. Be careful not to get any water in the pudding.

6. Bake the pudding for 45 minutes to 1 hour, or until the custard puffs up slightly and is lightly browned. During the last 35 minutes of baking, cover with foil.

7. Remove from oven and let cool for 10 minutes.

8. Spoon the pudding onto serving plates, drizzle with the Michigan Maple Crème Anglaise, and serve.

Use a good bread, such as brioche, French, wheat, or cinnamon.

Michigan Maple Crème Anglaise

1   cup milk
¼   cup heavy whipping cream
1   vanilla bean, split and scraped of seeds, **or** 1 teaspoon vanilla extract
4   large egg yolks
¼   cup sugar
½   cup maple syrup

1. In the top half of a double boiler, bring the milk, cream, and vanilla to a boil, stirring constantly. Reduce the heat and simmer for 3-4 minutes.

2. In a medium bowl, whisk together the egg yolks and sugar.

3. Stir ¼ cup of the warm milk mixture into the egg mixture. Then, pour the entire egg mixture into the double boiler mixture. Mix thoroughly over medium to low heat for 4 minutes, stirring constantly until the mixture lightly coats the back of a wooden spoon.

4. Remove the sauce from the heat and strain it into a medium bowl, using a mesh strainer to remove any particles of cooked egg. Whisk in the maple syrup in a steady stream.

Piña Colada Cheesecake

I learned to prepare this cheesecake while in Hawaii. A lovely chef, Kathleen Dalmens, taught me to prepare it while we were filming a television show.

1¾ cups graham cracker crumbs
½ teaspoon cinnamon
3 tablespoons maple syrup
6 egg whites
2 8-oz packages cream cheese, softened
1 cup sugar
¼ cup unsweetened crushed pineapple, strained
2 teaspoons pure vanilla extract
2 teaspoons coconut extract
pinch of salt
3 cups sour cream
Crushed Pineapple Topping

1. Preheat oven to 375.°

2. In a medium bowl, combine the graham cracker crumbs, cinnamon and maple syrup; mix thoroughly. Press into a 9″ springform pan. Chill ready to use.

3. In a large bowl, combine egg whites, cream cheese, sugar, pineapple, vanilla, coconut extract and salt; blend until smooth. Stir in sour cream. Pour into prepared piecrust and bake for 35 to 45 minutes, or until set. The filling will appear soft yet firm. Allow to sit at room temperature for one hour before adding topping.

4. Spread the Crushed Pineapple Topping over cheesecake. Chill in the refrigerator for 3 to 4 hours until set.

Crushed Pineapple Topping

1 cup crushed pineapple with juice
1 tablespoon cornstarch dissolved in 2 tablespoons warm water

1. Heat the pineapple in a small saucepan over medium heat until simmering. Add cornstarch mixture; and continue to stir until thickened.

2. Remove from heat and cool.

Note: It's easy to make this a fat-free dessert. Simply substitute low fat cream cheese and fat-free sour cream and you've got yourself a wonderful little treat.

Chocolate Pasta   Serves 2

¼   cup sugar
½   cup flour
1   tablespoon cocoa powder
¼   cup milk
1   egg, lightly beaten
¼   cup water
2   teaspoons melted butter
    vegetable oil
2   cups strawberries or blueberries
½   cup toasted almonds, chopped
1   cup chocolate sauce, your favorite
1   cup **Crème Anglaise**

1. Mix the sugar, flour, and cocoa powder together in a large bowl. Add the milk, egg, and ¼ cup water and blend well. Stir in the melted butter and place in the refrigerator for 30 minutes.

2. Strain the batter through a fine sieve into a large bowl.

3. Heat a nonstick sauté pan over medium heat; add a small amount of oil to the pan. Ladle ¼ cup of batter into the pan, enough to cover the bottom of the pan. Cook for 1 to 2 minutes; turn and cook for 1 or 2 minutes more. Repeat with remaining batter.

4. Let the crepes cool; do not stack. Store in the refrigerator until ready to serve.

5. To make the pasta: Julienne the crepes and divide the "pasta" onto the serving plates. Garnish with fresh berries, toasted almonds, Crème Anglaise, and your favorite chocolate sauce.

Crème Anglaise

1   cup milk
¼   cup heavy whipping cream
1   vanilla bean, split and scraped of seeds, **or** 1 teaspoon vanilla extract
4   large egg yolks
¼   cup sugar

1. In the top half of a double boiler, bring the milk, cream, and vanilla to a boil, stirring constantly. Reduce the heat and simmer for 3-4 minutes.

2. In a medium bowl, whisk together the egg yolks and sugar. Stir ¼ cup of the warm milk mixture into the egg mixture. Then, pour the entire egg mixture into the double boiler mixture. Mix thoroughly over medium to low heat for 4 minutes, stirring constantly, until the mixture lightly coats the back of a wooden spoon.

3. Remove the sauce from the heat and strain it into a medium bowl, using a mesh strainer to remove any particles of cooked egg.

Grilled Fruit with Tuaca and Tortilla Crunch Topping

Serves 4

½ pineapple, skinned, cored, and sliced into ½″ pieces
1 banana, sliced lengthwise
1 Granny Smith apple, cored and cut into ½″ circles
1 peach, cut into ½″ slices
1 plum, cut into ½″ slices
1 mango, peeled and cut lengthwise
2 large strawberries cut lengthwise
Tuaca Marinade
Tortilla Crunch Topping
1 cup heavy cream, whipped to soft peaks

1. Place fruit in a large bowl and pour the marinade over the fruit. Soak for 20 minutes.

2. Place the marinated fruit on a grill rack and grill over medium-high heat on both sides, until done, approximately 5 to 7 minutes.

3. Transfer fruit to a serving plate. Spoon whipped cream over the fruit and top with the Tortilla Crunch Topping.

Tuaca Marinade

½ cup Tuaca liqueur
3 tablespoons freshly squeezed orange juice
¼ cup brown sugar

Mix all ingredients together in a small bowl.

Tortilla Crunch Topping

4 flour tortillas
canola oil spray
cinnamon/sugar mixture

1. Preheat oven to 350.°

2. Julienne 4 flour tortillas. Place in a bowl and spray with a little canola oil. Sprinkle to taste with granulated sugar and cinnamon.

3. Place the tortillas on a sheet pan and bake in oven until they are browned and crispy. Set aside.

Poached Pear with White Chocolate Mousse

Serves 4

3   quarts water
7   cups sugar
    juice of one lemon
1   vanilla bean
4   pears, peeled
    White Chocolate Mousse
½   cup semisweet chocolate pieces
    Crème Anglaise
    fresh fruit for garnish
    pistachios, chopped for garnish

1. In a large saucepan, combine 3 quarts water, sugar, lemon juice, and vanilla bean and simmer on low heat for 30 minutes. Place peeled pears into liquid and poach for 15 minutes, or until a toothpick can be easily inserted into the side of a pear. Remove from heat and transfer pears and liquid to a bowl. Cool.

2. Remove the pears from the liquid and, using a melon baller, remove the core of the pear. Fill the pears with White Chocolate Mousse.

3. Place a pear in the center of each serving plate. Slowly melt the semisweet chocolate pieces in a double boiler. Dip a fork into melted chocolate and drizzle chocolate over the pears.

4. Spoon Crème Anglaise around each pear. Garnish with fresh fruit and chopped pistachios.

White Chocolate Mousse

⅓   lb white Callebaut® chocolate, melted
⅓   lb Nestle's® white chocolate, ground
⅓   cup sugar
4   egg whites
1⅓ pints heavy whipping cream, whipped to soft
    peaks.

1. Mix the melted chocolate and ground chocolate together by hand.

2. Dissolve the sugar and egg white in a double boiler. Remove from heat and whip until stiff. Gently fold chocolate into the egg whites, followed by whipped cream.

Crème Anglaise

1   cup milk
¼   cup heavy whipping cream
1   vanilla bean, split and scraped of seeds, **or** 1
    teaspoon vanilla extract
4   large egg yolks
¼   cup sugar

1. In the top half of a double boiler, bring the milk, cream, and vanilla to a boil, stirring constantly. Reduce the heat and simmer for 3-4 minutes.

2. In a medium bowl, whisk together the egg yolks and sugar. Stir ¼ cup of the warm milk mixture into the egg mixture. Then, pour the entire egg mixture into the double boiler mixture. Mix thoroughly over medium to low heat for 4 minutes, stirring constantly until the mixture lightly coats the back of a wooden spoon.

3. Remove the sauce from the heat and strain it into a medium bowl, using a mesh strainer to remove any particles of cooked egg.

My sincere gratitude to Nino Salvaggio and his wife Patti Kaye as well as the entire Nino Salvaggio staff in Rochester Hills, Michigan, for allowing us to take over the kitchen while preparing these recipes for the photo shoot.

Acknowledgments

Most of all, I wish to thank my mother for encouraging me, at the age of sixteen, to call Chef Duglass at the Great Dane to apply for a job. I love you.

I owe a great deal to Larry Wisne, owner of Chez Raphael, for his belief in my ability and support of my passion. I often fondly recall our menu sampling sessions. Thank you, Larry, you will forever remain very important to me.

Thanks to Chef Matt Prested, my special assistant for the projects I take on, including preparation of all of the recipes in *Famie's Adventures in Cooking* to be used in the photographs for this book. I can't live without you, Matt.

A special thanks to Chefs David Ogden and Todd Gardner. You've been with me through thick and thin. You're both destined for greatness.

The wine suggestions are courtesy of Maître'd Achille Bianchi of Too Chez (formerly Chez Raphael). Thanks; I miss you, friend.

Lisa Drum, of Crate & Barrel in Troy, Michigan very generously made all of the dinnerware available for the photo shoot. You're one in a million, Lisa.

My heartfelt appreciation to Christine Schefman, who had to decipher my difficult-to-read kitchen notes and recipes. Thanks, Christine.

A special thank you to my great Les Auteurs team: my Sous Chef, Shawn Loving, a passionate chef who could always keep me inspired; managers John Baumgartner, and John Messina, a great friend who helped make a challenging transition from Les Auteurs to Durango; Maître'd Michael Chamas who took over when Michael Morsette moved to the West Coast; my brother Randy, who always kept track of the finances; one of Detroit's finest pastry chefs, Ralph Macioce; Sous Chefs Donna Brown, and Rob Welker; Chef Robert Tubbs, the answer to my prayers on our Paris adventure; Chef Randy Emert, who followed me from Chez Raphael and is now one of the Detroit area's leading chefs; and Chef Eddie Matteson who faithfully remained at my side as my Chef de Cuisine and held down the fort in some of our toughest storms. Also, my close friend, Master Chef Jeff Gabriel, who helped out one long season. Two of my partners in particular, Ed Lundy and Don Tocco, you remain an inspiration.

Many thanks to my attorney, Steve Cole, accountant Larry Dzendzel, Chef Michael Berand, Sharon Bartlet, J. Burns and Pastry Chef Dallas Newman.

Finally, I thank you, the reader. This collection represents many years of my life, preparing foods for great friends and patrons. Bon Appetit!

Photo Credits: Beth Singer - pages 10 and 11, Patrick Gloria - page 142.